Rainer Maria Rilke

Said It Aloud And Heard It Die Away:
Rilke's Poems to Orpheus

Translated by
Frank Scalambrino

Castalia, OH: Magister Ludi Press
MMXX

Castalia, OH: Magister Ludi Press.
Scalambrino, Frank
ISBN: 978-1-947674-82-0 (Paperback)
ISBN: 978-1-947674-03-5 (Ebook)
1. Rilke (Poetry) 2. Orpheus (Philosophy) 3. Existentialism (Philosophy) 4. Scala Amoris (Platonic Metaphysics)

12 11 10 9 8 7 6 5 4

No matter

What has happened

No matter

Where you are

While I still have the eyes with which

To look back at you

While I still have the lips with which

To tell you...

I love you.

Said It Aloud
And Heard It
Die Away

I. (1907)
Orpheus, Eurydice, Hermes

This was the mysterious mine of souls.   **1**
Like silent silver ore, they wandered
through its dark veins. Through the roots rose blood,
toward human generations, and in the darkness
it looked heavy as fiery igneous rock.
Nothing else was red.

There were cliffs there
and phantasmagoric twilight forests. There were bridges
spanning the void, and that great gray blind lake
which hung above its distant bottom   **10**
like a rainy sky over a landscape.
And through the meadows, gentle and full of patience,
one pale path unrolling like a strip of cotton.

Down this path they were coming.

In front, the slender man in the blue cloak,
mute, impatiently looking straight ahead.
His stride devoured the path
in large unchewed bites; his hands hung
out of the falling folds heavy and closed   **20**
and no longer aware of the delicate stringed-instrument,
which had grown into his left arm like a vine of roses grafted
onto the branch of an olive tree.

His senses seemed as though they were divided:
his sight would race ahead of him like a dog,
stop, come back, then rushing off again
would stand waiting at the next turn, –
while his hearing, like an odor, stayed behind.
Sometimes it seemed to him as though it reached back
to the footsteps of those other two who were to follow him, the
whole ascent.   31
Then again, it was only his climb's echo
and his cloak in the wind that made the sound.

He said to himself, they had to be behind him;   34
said it aloud and heard it die away.
They had to be behind him,
but their steps were torturously soft. If only he could turn
around, just once, (but would looking back
not decompose this entire work, so near completion), surely he
would see them,
the two softly following him:

The god of passage rites and distant messages,   42
a traveler's hood above his brilliant eyes,
a slender staff held in front of him,
and wings fluttering at his ankles;
and presenting with his left hand: she.

So beloved was she, that from one stringed-instrument
more lament came than ever from lamenting women;
that a world of lament was made, where
everything was once again there: 50

Forest and valley and path and village, field and river and
animals; and that around this lament-world, just as
around the other earth, revolved a sun
and a starry silent heaven, a lament-heaven with displaced
stars –: This so beloved.

But now she walked by the god's hand,
her steps constricted by the trailing grave clothes, uncertain,
gentle, and without impatience.
She was within herself, like a secret anticipation,   **60**
and oblivious,
remained unaware of the procession, or the path ascending
into life.
She was within herself. Being dead filled her
beyond fulfillment.
Like the sweet darkness of a fruit spreading to its core.
She was filled with the vastness of death,
which was so new, she was not yet aware.

She was in a new virginity
and untouchable; her sex was closed   **69**
like a young flower at nightfall,
and her hands were so weaned from marriage,
that the god's infinitely gentle, guiding touch hurt her
like too much familiarity.

She was no longer the woman, echoing in the poet's song, **75**
no longer the bed's scent which urged him
to take her again
like a wave crashing against the shore.
She was no longer his.

She was already loosened like long hair
and poured out like fallen rain
and shared like a limitless supply.

She was already root.   82

Suddenly and abruptly
the god turned around and with grief in his voice spoke the
words: He has turned around –,
but she could not understand
and softly answered: Who?

Far away, dark before the radiant clearing,   87
was someone whose face was not visible.
He stood and saw, how on the strip of meadow path
with a mournful look
the god of messages silently turned,
to follow the shape, already descending
along the same path,   93
her steps constricted by the trailing grave clothes, uncertain,
gentle, and without impatience.

"Orpheus in the Underworld"
Oil painting by Jean Delville (1896)

II. (1922) Sonnets to Orpheus

§1 *1st Series – Sonnet 1*

There rose a tree. Such pure rising!
Ah! Orpheus Sings! How high this tree climbs in the ear!
Everything has stilled. Yet, in the silence
signs of a new beginning beckon, and change appears.

Silent animals appear in the clearing
inhabitants of this enchanted forest;
and, as it turned out, their silence
was not out of cunning or fear,

rather it was out of listening. Howling, shrieking, roaring
heeled in their hearts. And where
there was barely a dwelling to receive this,

the entrance to a longing hidden-away
in the darkness trembled, –
there you made them temples
in their capacity for sound.

§2 *1st Series – Sonnet 2*

And she was almost a girl who rose
from this harmony of song and lyre
glowing translucent through the veil of her spring shroud
she made herself a bed inside my ear.

And slept in me. And all in her sleep.
The trees, I admired,
this palpable distance,
the feeling of the meadow
and all the mysteries that filled me with awe.

The world in her slumber. Singing god,
how did you accomplish her
not wanting to be awake? See, she rose and slept.

Where is her death? Will you still compose
this theme before your song's expiration? –
To where does she sink from me? ... This almost girl.

§3 *1st Series – Sonnet 3*

A god can do it. But tell me, how
should a man follow after him
through the narrow lyre?
His mind is divided. At the intersection
of two heart paths where
there stands no temple for Apollo.

For singing, as you remind us, isn't desire,
it is not a plea for some end to be accomplished;
Singing is being. And, light for a god.
Yet, when *are* we? And, when does *he* turn

the earth and the stars around our being?
It *is* not, when you are young, that you love,
even if the voice opens your mouth – learn...

Forget that you sang. Those fleeting songs.
For the truth of singing, is another breath.
A breath of nothing. A god's mournful expiration. A wind.

§4 *1st Series – Sonnet 4*

O you tender ones, from time to time
step into a breath that is not yours,
let it divide as you face it,
and, trembling, behind you, reunite.

O you blessed ones, about to be healed,
for you the heart's beginning appears.
Bows for arrows and targets for arrows,
tear-stained your smile will shine eternally.

Do not avoid the pain, suffer its gravity,
let it return to the earth;
heavy are the mountains, heavy the sea.

Even those planted as children, the trees,
have long since become too grave, for you to sustain.
And, yet, this wind... These open spaces...

§5 *1st Series – Sonnet 5*

Erect no gravestone. Only leave the rose
blooming every year in memory of him.
Because Orpheus is. His metamorphosis
as this and this. We shouldn't struggle

to find another name. As if to capture in stone,
for, the song, is Orpheus. He comes and goes.
Isn't it enough, now and then,
for him to outlive the bouquet of roses?

O how it must evanesce, so that you'll understand!
And even if he were also afraid, that he might vanish.
As his every word surpasses being here,

he is there, where she cannot go.
Yet, the lattice of the lyre does not force his hand.
This transcendence is not transgression.

§6 *1st Series – Sonnet 6*

Is he from here? No, out of both
realms his vast nature grows.
To perfectly bend the branches of the willows
one must fully understand their roots.

When you go to bed, leave
neither bread nor milk on the table; attracting the dead –
Leave it to the conjuror
under the mildness of your eyelids

to combine their appearance with what lies in your view;
the magic of poppies and diamonds was as true to him
as the clearest glance.

Nothing can tarnish this enchanted vista;
whether from graves or gathering places,
let him eulogize jar, necklace, and ring.

§7 *1st Series – Sonnet 7*

Eulogy, that's it! Called to eulogize,
he rose and flowed
like silent silver ore from stone. His heart,
ah, a fleeting wine press of never-ending wine,
for us alone.

His voice never fails, singing amongst the dirt,
when the divine instance affects him.
All becomes vineyard, all becomes grape,
fermenting in a soul-filled South.

Neither mold in royal tombs,
nor a shadow falling from the gods,
could make his praise a lie.

He is one of the messengers who remains,
holding open the doors of the dead
overflowing containers with glorious fruit.

§8 *1st Series – Sonnet 8*

Only in the space of lament can such praise
flow, for the nymph at the spring of tears,
oversees the splashing descent of our cascade,
that it arrives clear on the same rock.

That sustains gates and altars.
See, around her still shoulders blooms
the feeling, that she is the youngest
among the siblings of the mind.

Exultation *knows*, and yearning confesses, –
only lament still learns; girlish
night after night she counts the ancient sorrows.

Yet, suddenly, with inexperienced reflection,
she holds a constellation of voice
up to a sky unclouded by her breath.

§9 *1st Series – Sonnet 9*

Only one who has already raised the lyre
among shadows too,
may have a presentiment
of the proffered infinite praise's return.

Only one who has dined with the dead,
on their own poppies,
will never again forget
the quietest of tones.

Although the pond's reflection
often blurs us
know the image.

It is only in the lament-world
where voices become gentle
and eternal.

§10 *1st Series – Sonnet 10*

With you, who never left my feelings,
I greet, ancient tombs,
the joyful water of romantic days
as a wandering song flows through you.

Or those as open as the pupils
of a joyful waking shepherd
– overflowing with silence and honeysuckle –
around which enchanted butterflies flutter;

of all those freed from doubt
I greet, the mouths reopened
after learning the meaning of silence.

Do we know, friends, or do we not?
That which shapes this lesson in hesitation
as the features of a human face.

§11 *1st Series – Sonnet 11*

Look among the stars. Is no constellation called "Rider"?
For we share much with the proud earth:
to which it is peculiarly emblazed.
And, with a second, who drives and reins him
and whom he carries.

Isn't this, first hunted and then tamed,
the nature of this be-ing strung together?
Path and turn. Awareness of urgency.
New expanse. And the two are one.

But are they? Or do they both intend
not this path, they travel together?
Even without a name, it separates house and meadow.

For, celestial connections can also be misleading.
But we are happy for a while now,
to believe the figure. That is enough.

§12 *1st Series – Sonnet 12*

Praise the spirit, that may connect us;
for truly we live in figures.
And clocks, with small steps, move
alongside our actual day.

Without really knowing where we are,
we act as if these references are real.
We feel what we can,
and are carried an empty distance...

Pure suspense. Ah, the power of music!
Do our trivial concerns not interfere
with your remote transmission?

Even if the farmer cares and acts,
where the seed transforms in summer,
he cannot reach it. The earth gives.

§13 *1st Series – Sonnet 13*

Fully-ripe apple, pear, and banana,
gooseberry... All of these reveal
death and life through the mouth... Envision it...
See it in a child's face,

as it tastes them. It comes from afar.
In your mouth, is an ineffability slowly growing?
Where there once were words, now flows
mysteries freed from pulp.

Dare to say, the meaning of apple.
This sweetness, which quickly intensifies
silently elevating in the taste,

waking, becoming clear and transparent,
double meaning of this earthy, sunny, here:
Oh experience, feeling, joy – immensity!

§14 *1st Series – Sonnet 14*

We dwell among blooms, leaves and fruit.
They speak not only an annual language.
Their colorful manifestation rises
from a darkness which may shine

with the jealousy of the dead,
whose luster refreshes the earth.
What do we know of their part in this?
Since time immemorial, it has been their nature, the clay
which is their manifestation to style.

The only question now: Do you dwell so willingly? ...
The urges of such fruit, a work of heavy enslavement,
does it embrace us, as its master?

Or are they the master's, roots in their graves,
treating us with their abundance
a silent mixture of power and kisses?

§15 *1st Series – Sonnet 15*

Wait... this flavor... Already dying away.
... Piece of music, tapping feet, a hum –:
Young women inflaming you with their silence,
dance the experience of the taste of fruit!

Dance the orange. Who can forget her,
the way she labors, drowning in herself
resisting her sweetness. You possessed her.
She transformed for you deliciously.

Dance the orange. Its warmer landscape
cast it out of you, so that its ripeness may shine
in the midst of its nativity. Peel away

each glowing note of its fragrance! Intercourse
with its purity, with the resistance of its flesh,
with the joy of the flavorful juice inside!

§16 *1st Series – Sonnet 16*

You, my friend, are lonely because...
With pointing fingers and words
we gradually make the world our own,
perhaps the weakest, most dangerous part.

Who points a finger at a scent?
Yet of the mysterious forces, that threaten us,
you can feel many... You know the dead,
and you shrink away from the conjuror's charm.

Look, now our undertakings are the same
dealt a puzzle of fragments and parts, as if it were a whole.
Helping you will be difficult. Above all: Plant

me not in your heart. I would grow too fast.
And yet, I will guide *my* master's hand and say:
Erotic love is no hoax.

§17 *1st Series – Sonnet 17*

At bottom the oldest, convoluted,
all the uplifting
roots, the hidden spring
never gazed upon.

War paint and battle cries,
nostalgia of the elders,
strife among men,
the sounds of women...

Growing, branches compel branches,
not one of them free...
Yet, this one! Rise... Oh, rise...

For, they all still break.
Yet, this one above
bends into a lyre.

§18 *1st Series – Sonnet 18*

Do you hear the new, Orpheus,
resounding and trembling?
Approaching heralds
uplift it.

No hearing is untouched
in the frenzy,
yet the automated part
now wants to be honored.

See, the machine:
how it wreaks havoc and venges
and distorts and weakens us.

It gets its force from us,
it, without passion,
compels and serves.

§19 *1st Series – Sonnet 19*

The world is also changing rapidly
like cloud shapes,
everything accomplished recycles
homeward to the oldest.

Above what's changing and passing,
your overture endures,
wider and freer,
god with the lyre.

Suffering not yet understood,
love has not been learned,
and what removes us in death

is not yet unveiled.
Only the song over the Earth
praises and celebrates.

§20 *1st Series – Sonnet 20*

Yet, to you, Orpheus, what could I dedicate?
You who teach all creatures to hear, tell me
I remember the evening
of a spring day, far away, and a horse...

In solitude, he traversed the village,
his fettered leg trailing a stake,
to be alone in the meadow at night;
how his curly mane shook against his neck,

keeping time with the rhythm of his high spirits
indifferent to his inhibited gallop.
With surging stallion-blood, oh how he leapt!

For, he felt the vast openness, and whether
he sang and heard – he was closed within
your call-and-response song.
                    His image: I dedicate to you.

§21 *1st Series – Sonnet 21*

Spring has come again. The earth overflows
like a child, reciting poems by heart;
many, so many... and through this appeal,
against such long painful lessons, is rewarded.

Such severe lessons. Though the snowy white
was like a wise teacher's beard.
Now, we can ponder the green and blue:
Yes, she can, she was made for it, she can!

Earth, set free, ecstatic, play
with your children now. We want to capture you
cheerful earth. To the most cheerful goes the reward.

All the lessons she has received, so many,
all that's imprinted in roots and etched in
rising branches: She sings it, now she sings!

§22 *1st Series – Sonnet 22*

We are the driving force.
Yet the pace of time,
is merely a trifle compared
to what is always there.

All that is hastening
soon will be gone;
for only what endures
first makes us one.

Youth, don't trade
your courage for speed.
All that is happening
has already happened.

All is still:
Dark and light,
flowers and books.

§23 *1st Series – Sonnet 23*

Only *then*, when the flight
itself sufficient
no longer for its own sake
ascends into the heavenly stillness,

shining forth again,
as that instrument, that succeeded,
to be darling plaything of the wind,
slender and confidently swaying –

only when a pure whither
means more than a youth-filled
pride in swelling machines,

will one, spurred by gain, become
near to that which is distant, and
be, the lonely flight's end.

§24 *1st Series – Sonnet 24*

Should we reject our age-old friendship
with the great gods who have ceased to recruit us,
because the hardness of our training does not know them,
or should we suddenly search for them on a map?

These powerful friends, who take the dead from us,
never even brush against us.
Our baths and our feasts take place too far away
from their messengers, who have long been too slow for us,

we always overtake. More lonely now
wholly dependent on each other, yet not knowing each other,
we no longer traverse the paths as beautiful meanders,
rather we travel in calculated degrees.

The former fires only burn now in factories,
raising instruments which are getting bigger and bigger.
Yet we are losing strength like swimmers.

§25 *1st Series – Sonnet 25*

You, whom I knew like a flower whose name
I didn't know, you were about to evaporate.
I will remember you, now, one last time,
and describe you to them, beautiful playmate
of the insurmountable scream.

Dancer, whose body hesitated, and paused
suddenly, as if her youth were being cast in bronze;
grieving and listening. Then, from the great creators
music fell into her transformed heart.

Death was near. Already besieged by shadows,
darkening her blood, and yet, as we momentarily expected,
it pulsed on into its natural springtime.

Again and again, interrupted by darkness and fall,
it shone-forth, earthly. Until after a terrible throbbing
it stepped through the bleakly open gate.

§26 *1st Series – Sonnet 26*

And yet, you, divine one, resounding until the end,
since the swarm of spurned maenads attacked,
you drowned out their shrieks with order, you beautiful one,
your voice rose from the chaos of your destroyers.

Not one of them could destroy your head or lyre,
however much they violently raged;
and all the sharp stones they threw at your heart
upon touching you turned tender,
suddenly gifted with hearing, they heard your song.

Enraged with vengeance, at last they broke and tore you,
while your sound still echoed in lions and rocks
and in the trees and birds. You still sing now.

Oh you lost god! You infinite trail!
Since hatred finally dismembered you,
now we are the ears and mouth of nature.

§27 *2nd Series – Sonnet 1*

Breathing, you invisible poem!
Rendering, the whole time
be-ing a pure exchange of outer space. Counterpoint,
in which I come to be rhythm.

Solitary wave, whose
gradual sea I am;
most measured of all possible seas, –
surplus space.

How many of these constellations of space have already been
inside me. Many winds
are like my children.

Do you know me, air? Still full of my memories,
will you remember me? You who were once
the bark, trunk, and greenery of my words.

§28 *2nd Series – Sonnet 2*

Sometimes, just as the nearest piece of paper
is canvas to masterful work: so too mirrors
can capture divinity in the smile of a girl,

in the experience of morning, alone –
or in the glow of attending candle lights.
Afterward, real and breathing faces later show
mere reflection.

What have eyes looking into the glow
of a slow-dying fire seen:
glimpses of a life, lost forever.

Ah, who understands the earth's losses?
Only the one who can, undeterred,
sing his heart into all this death.

§29 *2nd Series – Sonnet 3*

Mirrors: no description has yet beheld,
what you are in your essence.
You, fill openings in time
like holes in a sieve.

You, still squander the empty room –,
when it dawns like twilight over the forest...
or when the luster leaves like a trophy stag leaping,
beyond the bounds of your accessibility.

Sometimes you are full of images.
Some seem to have passed into you –,
others you shyly sent away.

Yet the most beautiful will remain,
until Narcissus finally irrupts
and conceals her chaste face.

§30 *2nd Series – Sonnet 4*

Oh, this is that beast, who never really is.
Not knowing it, they nonetheless watch it move
– its neck, its stance, its stride,
even the quiet look of its eyes – and love it.

It wasn't. Yet because they loved it,
it became a pure beast. They gave it room.
And in that room, clear and hollow,
it raised its head and scarcely needed anything

to be. They nourished it, not with grain,
merely with the possibility of being.
And that gave the beast such strength,

that a horn emerged from its brow. Unicorn.
All white, it showed up for a girl, and she perceived it –
in the silvery mirror and in her.

§31 *2nd Series – Sonnet 5*

Reflex of the flower, which slowly stretches open,
anemone to its meadow morning,
gradually opening up until,
the polyphonic light of the heavens bursts-forth,

pouring into the silent flower star,
tensely quivering in an infinite reception,
sometimes so overwhelmed,
even the withdrawing calm

barely allows the spread open petals
to retain their edges: you,
the will and power of how many worlds!

We violent men, we last longer.
Yet when, in what life,
are we at last open and receptive?

§32 *2nd Series – Sonnet 6*

Rose, enthroned, from ancient times
you were a calyx with a simple brim.
For us you are the innumerably full bloom,
the inexhaustible thing.

In your wealth you enwrap like raiment
to drape a body of nothing but splendor;
yet your every petal is at the same time the negation
and refusal of all clothing.

For centuries calling us your fragrance
its sweetest names cross over;
suddenly hanging in the air like glory.

Still, we don't know what to call it, we guess...
And memory proceeds to carry over,
what we requested from effable hours.

§33 *2nd Series – Sonnet 7*

Flowers, finally akin to the hands that arranged them,
(hands of women first and hands of women now),
laid on the garden table often from end to end,
gently wounded, wilting, spent,

waiting for the water to rescue her once more
from her death already begun – and now
again taken up between the opposing, sorting fingers

accomplishing more than you can foresee,
as you recover in the vase, slowly cooling
the warmth of women, like a confession,

exuding from you, like dim fading sins
committed by your being plucked, and
a reference to your bond with them, your blooming.

§34 *2nd Series – Sonnet 8*

You few playmates, with whom I shared my life,
scattered across the city's gardens:
How we hesitantly found ourselves
well suited to each other, and
like the lamb with the blade,

silently spoke. When we were happy
no one owned it. Whose could it be?
And how it dissolved among the noise of others around us,
and the long year's anxiety.

Passing us by, strange vehicles,
houses surrounded us, solid but unreal – and none
ever knew us. What was real in all that?

Nothing. Only the celestial spheres. Their marvelous paths.
Not even the children... But sometimes one,
oh, a dying one, coupled with the trajectory
of a descending sphere.

§35 *2nd Series – Sonnet 9*

Do not boast, you judges, of unnecessary torture
that necks are no longer shackled by iron.
No one is comforted, no heart – because
a predestined spasm of tenderness distorts you.

What it through time received, the gallows returns
like children receiving their toys from a previous birthday.
Into the pure, the high, the open heart
the god of real tenderness would

enter differently. More powerfully, and grip you,
overflowing with godlike radiant light.
More than a wind for corpulent complacent ships.

Nothing less than the secret, slight awareness,
that silently wins us over, inside
like the child of an infinite coupling, playing quietly.

§36 *2nd Series – Sonnet 10*

Like a machine, all that we gain threatens us,
for tools propelled by the blind force of habit,
the marvelous hand no longer reveals resplendent
circumspection, efficiency eclipses more resolute building.

Nowhere does it stand aside, so we might escape it,
as if pausing to oil itself in a suddenly quiet factory.
It thinks it is alive – it thinks itself all-knowing,
and with the same determination orders
and creates and destroys.

Yet, existence for us is still enchanted; at a hundred
places it is still the origin. A playing of pure
powers, that no one touches, who does not kneel and marvel.

Hurled at the ineffable, words still turn tender...
And music, ever new, from the vibrant stones,
builds a temple in unusable space.

§37 *2nd Series – Sonnet 11*

As if death could be subjugated, mortals made rules,
like orderly standards for hunting;
yet, more than a trap or a net, I know you,
strips of cloth covering a sinkhole,

you were quietly let in as if you were a symbol
for honoring peace. And then: a would-be victim
surmounted your edges. – And out of the darkness
the night burst forth doves into the light...
                        Yet, even that, is as it should be.

Far from view there is a hint of regret,
and not only from the hunter,
whose actions, it turns out,
are timely and fatal.

Killing is a form of the grief of our wandering...
Yet, whatever happens to us
is pure in the radiant spirit.

§38 *2nd Series – Sonnet 12*

Want transformation. Ah, be crazed for the flame,
that which eludes you in it is a sign of transformation,
that designing spirit that masters the earth,
loves nothing more than the turning point.

Whatever is set upon enduring is already is dead;
does homely drabness feel like shelter?
"Beware," the petrified warn from the distance of their death.
                    Indeed – another mindless hammer is lifted!

He who pours himself out, is recognized as a source;
and she leads him enraptured through a joyous creation,
that often ends with beginning and begins with ending.

Every happy space, they ecstatically traverse,
is the child or grandchild of a previous separation.
To feel the laurel of the transformed Daphne,
you must evaporate into breeze.

§39 *2nd Series – Sonnet 13*

Be ahead of all departures, as if it were already
behind you, like the winter that's just past.
Though the winter may feel endless,
overwintering it, your heart overcomes it.

Be forever dead in Eurydice – singingly climb,
gratefully return to the pure harmony.
Here, among those who are dwindling,
be a glass that shatters as it sings.

Be – and at the same time know
the condition of not-being,
the infinite depth of your intimate vibration,
so that you can do it completely this time.

To nature's supply, of that which has been used,
to the empty and speechless
in the fullness of nature's incalculable sums,
add yourself, rejoicing, and nullify the account.

§40 *2nd Series – Sonnet 14*

See the flowers, faithful to earth's ways,
we attribute fate to them from the brink of fate –
And, yet, who knows! If they regret their withering,
their regret may be ours to feel.

Everything wants to glide. Yet we lumber about
as if delighted with the weight, we place on ourselves;
oh, what kind of model are we for the eternally childlike
things of nature?

If someone were to embrace their sleep,
deeply and intimately –: oh, how light he'd return,
changing with each day, out of a mutual depth.

Or, if he stayed with them, they would blossom
and praise him, as one transformed, now like them,
all the satisfied siblings, swaying in the wind of the meadow.

§41 *2nd Series – Sonnet 15*

Oh earth-spring, you giver, you mouth,
who speaks the inexhaustible oneness, purely –
you, mask of marble, covering the flowing
water's face. And the outlet

the aqueduct's origin. Far away, past graves,
from the slopes of the Italian mountains,
your words are brought to you, flowing
over your aged weathered chin

falling into the vessel in front of you.
This is the ear laid to the ground and asleep,
the marble ear into which you always speak.

An ear of the earth. She is always talking
only to herself. Filling your jug,
it seems to her that you're interrupting.

§42 *2nd Series – Sonnet 16*

Torn apart, again and again,
Orpheus is still the place of healing.
We are sharp because we want to know,
yet, even destroyed, he is serene and cheerful.

For, even the pure, sacred offering
he does not take into his world,
other than by turning
without movement, illuminating the free end.

Only the dead drink
from the source that's *heard* by us,
the god's silent waves to the dead
are a secret hint to us.

The dead offer us only noise.
And from a quieter instinct,
the lamb seeks out pure bells.

§43 *2nd Series – Sonnet 17*

Where, in which heavenly-watered gardens,
on which trees, from what lovingly unsheathed flower-calyxes
do the strange fruits of consolation ripen?
These exquisite ones, which you might find in the downtrodden

field of your poverty. Time after time you wonder about
the size of the fruit, the smoothness of its skin, and
that the carelessness of the bird nor the jealousy of the worm
did not anticipate its arrival.

Are there trees where angels gather,
tended by hidden gardeners, slowly and so strangely,
that they sustain us without being ours?

We have never been able, we shadows and specters,
as we hastily mature and then wither again,
to disturb that calm tranquility of summer.

§44 *2nd Series – Sonnet 18*

Dancer: oh you translation
of all that passes into steps: how would you put it?
And the whirl at the end, this tree of motion,
did it not assume possession of the entire year?

Didn't it blossom so your earlier swirl might
swarm around him, like an abrupt crowning of silence?
And this immeasurable warmth of yours,
above it, was there no sun, was it not summer?

Yet, he also produced, he produced, your tree of ecstasy.
Are these not its quiet fruits: the jug, streaked ripe,
and the vase even riper?

And in these images: doesn't the sketch endure,
your eyebrows, streaked, as if, on the wall of your memory,
was quickly scrawled your turning.

§45 *2nd Series – Sonnet 19*

The gold resides somewhere in the decadent bank,
and is on intimate terms with the pampered masses.
But for the blind beggar, a copper coin is like a place
that is lost, an inaccessible dusty corner.

All along the shops, money seems right at home,
and apparently dresses up in silk, carnations, and fur.
He, the silent one, stands in the pauses
of all the breathing that money makes, asleep or awake.

Oh, how she may close at night, this always open hand.
Fate will bring it again tomorrow, and every day
it holds it out: vivid, wretched, unending destruction.

If only some onlooker, repulsed, sung of this persistence.
Yet, it is only visible to artists.
And only audible to a god.

§46 *2nd Series – Sonnet 20*

Between the stars, how far; and yet, how much further
what one learns here.
One, for example, a child... and, then, another –
oh how incomprehensibly removed.

Fate, perhaps it measures us
with a such span of be-ing,
that it seems strange to us;
think, of the span alone between woman and man
as she entices and avoids him.

Everything is distant – and nowhere is the circle closed.
See, on the festive table, on the dish,
how strange the faces of fish.

Fish are dumb... or so we think. Who knows?
Isn't there a place where they communicate?
And, can that language be spoken without them?

§47 *2nd Series – Sonnet 21*

Sing, my heart, of gardens you've never known;
like gardens cast on glass, clearly, unattainable.
Water and roses from grapes or gardens,
sing them blissfully, praise them, as incomparable.

Show, my heart, that you are not for a moment without them.
That it is you their ripening figs have in mind.
That you travel with the breezes between their pregnant stems,
frenzied to the point of a vision.

Avoid the mistake of believing
that you are being deprived, that you have offended fate,
by your decision: to be!
For, you are the silk thread woven into the fabric.

Whatever image is most inwardly yours
(even if only a moment in a life of pain)
feel, that the whole is the meaning
of this glorious fatal tapestry.

§48 *2nd Series – Sonnet 22*

Oh, despite fate: the glorious abundance of our existence,
foaming over in parks and splendid estates –
or as stone men propping up lofty balconies over tall entrances!

Oh, the brass bell, swinging its cudgel daily
against the drudge of everyday life.
Or the one pillar, in the Egyptian Karnak Complex,
that has outlived the temples built for eternity.

Today, these same surpluses, hurry past us,
from the horizontal yellow day
into a polluted, heavily over-lit, night.

Yet, the frenzy passes and leaves no trace.
Curves of flight through the air and those who control them,
though none may be meaningless, they are never quite real.

§49 *2nd Series – Sonnet 23*

Call me at that hour of yours,
that continues to resist you:
pleading close as the face of a dog,
yet always turned away,

when you think it is finally caught.
What is taken like this is most yours.
We are free. For we were dismissed,
right where we thought ourselves welcomed.

Afraid, we reach out only for a hold,
sometimes, we're too young for what is old,
and too old for that which never was.

We are only where we praise nonetheless.
Because, oh, we are the knot and the blade,
and the sweetness of a ripening hazard.

§50 *2nd Series – Sonnet 24*

Oh, this pleasure, always feels new, of loosened clay!
Almost no one helped the earliest explorers.
Yet, cities still emerged from blissful bays,
water and oil still filled the jugs.

Gods, we make bold plans with grand designs,
that seemingly mercurial fate eventually destroys.
It is they, though, who are the immortals.
See, we should listen to the one
who will finally hear us in the end.

We, one generation through millennia: mothers and fathers,
more and more fulfilled by future offspring,
who will, one day, overtake us, later.

We, we children of endless hazard, what time do we have!
And it is only silent death, who knows what we are,
and what he continually wins, when he lends us to life.

§51 *2nd Series – Sonnet 25*

Listen, already, you can hear the work of the initial rake over;
again the human rhythm measures the silence
of the fertile early spring earth. And what has come before

seems to return as fresh as ever. That which has come
to you so often seems to come again like new.
What you always hoped for, you never captured.
It captured you.

Even the leaves of wintered oaks
shine a future brown in the evening.
Sometimes the breeze gives a signal.

The shrubs are black. Yet heaps of manure
collect in the fields, an even richer black.
Each passing hour grows younger.

§52 *2nd Series – Sonnet 26*

How we are moved by the call of a bird...
Or any newly-created cry.
Yet already the children are, playing in the open air,
drowning out real cries...

Chance cries. Into the spaces between, into time,
(a space meant for bird cries, where men go into dreams)
cries driven like wedges.

Oh, where are we? Ever less fettered,
like kites torn free, tattered by the wind,
laughing at the edges of our windy shreds.

Order their cries, singing god! that they wake
resounding like the current
carrying the head and the lyre.

§53 *2nd Series – Sonnet 27*

Does time truly exist? Does it actually annihilate?
When, on the resting mountain, does it break the castle?
This heart, infinitely belonging to the gods,
when will time overcome it?

Are we really as frightened and fragile,
as fate sometimes seems to suggest?
Is childhood, so deep, and full of promise,
in its roots – later – silenced?

Oh, the fear of impermanence,
like a phantom, passes through the unsuspecting,
as if it were smoke.

As for us, the ones who strive,
among the permanent forces,
we have our divine use.

§54 *2nd Series – Sonnet 28*

Oh, come and go, you, almost still a child, for a moment,
intensify the dance figure of the pure constellation
in one of those dances with which, though transient, we

transcend the dead order of nature.
For she only listens completely when Orpheus sings.
It was you who was inspired at that time,
and slightly surprised when any tree hesitated

before joining you in the rhythms. You still knew
the place where the lyre rose;
– the unheard-of center.

So you, lovingly, translatingly danced, hoping
to attract the look and step of your friend
into the sacred celebration.

§55 *2nd Series – Sonnet 29*

Silent friend of many distances, feel,
how your breath is still making space.
Bell-like, let it ring you through
the dark bell towers. Whatever preys

on you will grow strong from this nourishment.
Know transformation through and through.
What is your most suffering experience?
Turn, if drinking's bitter, into wine.

Be in this vast night
the magic power at your senses' intersection,
the truth of their strange encounter.

And if you the earthly no longer remembers
say to the still-silent earth: I flow.
To the rushing water speak: I am.

III. Seven Straightforward Comments with which to Understand the Mysteries of Orpheus & Eurydice

My hope for this section is simply to provide a few straightforward, simple, statements to begin to illuminate the Mysteries of Orpheus & Eurydice for readers.

§1 *If Being Embodied is a Kind of After Life and Death for the Soul, then the Physical Dimension is the Deathlands, the Underworld*

According to Plato, initiates into the Sacred Mysteries seemed to understand the condition of having a body as a kind of death. Insofar as we recognize this, then all the various characterizations of the Underworld found in the myths may be understood as referring to the experience of the physical dimension.

§2 *When Eurydice Dies, She "Falls" into the Physical Dimension; She Falls into the Condition of Having a Terrestrial Body*

Just as a constellation of stars can be seen from many different points of view on the earth, the light from the *one* constellation is contained in *many* eyes at once. It is in this way that human beings can participate in these mysteries. Notice that Orpheus retrieving Eurydice refers to extracting the light from the physical vessel in which it is entombed. The next two insights into the mysteries stem directly from this insight – the first regarding Orpheus, the second regarding the physical vessel.

§3 *Because Orpheus Figured Out How to Enter the Physical Dimension (the Underworld) and, then, Exit It, He Illuminates a Path Out of this Embodied Condition (Death)*

There are multiple endings to the Orpheus Myth. According to some Orpheus becomes a swan, to others he is torn apart (*sparagmos*) by the maenads, to others (see Rilke's 1907 poem) he is merely forced back out of the Underworld. Yet, it seems to me that perhaps all of these endings could coexist and accurately characterize the Orpheus Myth.

Since it would take us too far afield to discuss all of these endings and how they may coexist (though my *Meditations on Orpheus* may be helpful for anyone who wishes to push further into the more esoteric aspects of the Myth), the point we should emphasize here is that the journey of Orpheus, so to speak, illuminates a path of salvation and liberation from the "dead" condition of being embodied. Plato referred to that path as the *scala amoris*.

§4 *The Path out of the Underworld (the Scala Amoris) is a Path of Transformation Regarding the Experience of Love*

The experience of love in the Underworld is initially experienced *as* physicality. The ultimate idea here is that love is not a physical thing. However, we may think of it as, or believe it to be, a physical thing, given our embodied experience of it. Thus, the *scala amoris* refers to the revelation of love as spiritual, not physical. On the one hand, this revelation is experiential. And, it seems to me that it most definitely involves the influence of some awareness of death. This is because as we ascend the stairway of love (the *scala amoris*) we become aware of the potential loss of the beloved, of the object of our love. Of course, that is the en-trance of Orpheus.

On the other hand, this revelation is thoroughly psychological. In other words, the experience of ascending the *scala amoris* is a spiritual transformation that intimately involves our own psychological disposition. For, the transformation changes our relation to physicality. It changes how we see it, how we experience it, and it, of course, also changes how we see and experience others, the beloved, and the object of our love.

§5 *Ascending the Scala Amoris Coincides with Moving-through the Myth of Orpheus & Eurydice, and the Experience of Orpheus Involves the Activation of Divine Potential*

We know the general features of the Myth of Orpheus & Eurydice, so that's not the focus of this insight. What we want to focus on here is the changing experience of Orpheus, especially his experience of nearly retrieving Eurydice, looking back at her, and "losing" her forever.

I find it difficult to state this insight straightforwardly; however, the basic idea is that the belief in the reality of our subjectivity is associated more with the understanding of love as physical, rather than spiritual. Thus, as we climb the *scala amoris*, we begin to recognize that Orpheus is having the experience, not us. We begin to recognize the difference between the stars in the constellation and their reflection in our eyes.

This insight is difficult to simply unpack; that is, simply stating the truths associated with this ascension would be insufficient. The transformation comes from *the experience* and the truths manifest through the transformation. However, I will make some straightforward general comments regarding this insight.

Just as we begin to recognize that is it Orpheus who is having the experience, the divine potential involved here is our ability to see ourselves differently. It is as if the eyes become aware that they are merely witnessing a reflection on their surface. Just like the plants and trees and animals in the phantasmagoria of Orpheus' lament song, we respond. We enliven.

A transformation is affected through which we have the potential to recognize how our self-identity is tied to the various stages of the experience of Orpheus, and this awareness seems to coincide with the activation of the potential to experience reality differently. In other words, it is not simply that we see ourselves and the beloved and Orpheus differently, our experience of reality manifests in accord with the awareness.

§6 *Depending How We Navigate the Experience of Orpheus, He May Illuminate the Truth of this Embodiment (the Truth of Being Dead)*

What does it mean to just straightforwardly say that "our experience of reality" changes? Let's elucidate this in two ways. First, and foremost, we witness our experience of embodiment differently. I'm going to state this technically here, though if it doesn't make sense right now, don't worry, it will eventually make sense to you:

We come to see that the subject/object distinction is an abstract generalization manifesting from an understanding still fettered to the physical. As we awaken more in the transcendental dimension, our understanding also awakens. This is not an either/or, though. We can still understand our experience of reality in terms of subject/object, but we also understand it in a deeper and higher way.

Second, this deeper and higher understanding would be analogous to a flower becoming aware of its own blooming and understanding the pain in terms of the changes that must occur if the flower is to bloom. Put more directly, though still figuratively, it is as if the soul itself is waking from the slumber that accompanies entombment. Of course, we could also mention the figure Plato articulated in the *Phaedrus*, namely:

As the soul entombed in this body regrows its wings, its experience of the tomb and its understanding of its entombment change. With this in mind we may be able to see the deepest aspect of this insight. That is, our subjective understanding of our experience of reality depends on the extent to which we are still fettered in our tomb. This brings us to the deepest aspect of this insight, because it provides a revelation regarding death.

§7 *When the Soul Gains Awareness of the Truth of Its Death, It is Better Able to Harness Its Divine Potential and Free Itself From the Chains of this Embodiment*

We must keep in mind that there is a difference between, on the one hand, merely recognizing the meaning of these words and the logic by way of which they make sense and, on the other hand, the experience of these insights. The experience of these insights brings a new awareness that simply understanding the words and logic may not bring. Thus, the value of sympathizing (resonating) with the pain of Orpheus.

That being said, there is a reciprocal manifestation that results from ascending the *scala amoris*. I would prefer to state the insight into this reciprocal awareness in terms of the experience of time; however, doing so would no longer be so "straightforward," so I will state it along the same lines as the other insights.

On the one hand, the *experiential* awareness of embodiment as entombment in the Underworld manifests a change of relation to embodiment. However, this must be sincere. This is life or death; it's not simply a thought experiment. If you can't experience your embodiment this way, then what I'm saying here most likely sounds self-destructive. – *Evidently not everyone is capable of listening into the mysterious depths of the lament-song of Orpheus.* – Be this as it may, the change of relation to embodiment seems to open, otherwise eclipsed, potential.

On the other hand, the activation of this potential (and it seems as though the awareness of it is already the beginning of its activation) manifests itself as a kind of confirmation. In other words, recognizing the illusory nature of experience generalized in terms of subjectivity is like a kind of death. The identity associated with subjective experience dies. Of course, it can't really die because it was never really born; however, when we stop experiencing reality as if we are only that subject, then it may seem as though *the self that is the generalization of our subjective experience has died.*

Finally, then, all of this contributes what we may call here the "gaining of momentum" in regard to breaking free of one's fetters, of being liberated from one's entombment. Interestingly, these fetters are – of course, if you think about it – psychological. Transcending these psychological fetters and ascending the *scala amoris* (this involves intense emotional pain as per the *sparagmos* experience of Orpheus) manifests a new view of reality and experience of embodiment. This new view of reality and the new experience of embodiment, then, coincide with Orpheus' exit from the Underworld.

IV. Summary of the Orpheus Myth

> "When I behold, upon the night's starr'd face,
> Huge cloudy symbols of a high romance,
> And think that I may never live to trace
> Their shadows, with the magic hand of chance;
> And when I feel, fair creature of an hour,
> That I shall never look upon thee more..."
> ~John Keats, ("When I have fears")

§1 *The Celestial-Body of Orpheus*

A number of poets have attempted to render the Orpheus myth; most notably, Ovid (43 BC-17/18 AD) and Rainer Maria Rilke (1871-1926 AD). Orpheus, it seems, has always been thought of as the "patron saint" of poets and musicians, artists, and, ultimately, philosophers. Sometimes called "musician of the soul," Orpheus is often called upon in the high hope to be possessed by the divine manias of which Orpheus was said to embody (cf. Taylor, 1896: lii; cf. Plato, 1997g).

For example, in regard to Pindar's invocation we hear, "Orpheus is evidently to be seen as the mythical ancestor of the encomiastic [praise-giving orator] poet, and he may be regarded as a figure of identification for Pindar himself." (Kohnken, 2010: 146). From Isocrates in *Busiris* we are told, "Orpheus led the dead back from Hades" (Isocrates, 1945: p. 107). Further, Apollonius of Rhodes in *Argonautica* and Virgil in the *Georgics* provide consistent reference to Orpheus, and we find reference to him in Aeschylus, Sophocles, Aristophanes, and Euripides.

Frank Scalambrino

According to Sir William Smith's excellent (1876) *A Dictionary of Greek and Roman Biography and Mythology,*

> The history of the extant productions of Greek literature begins with the Homeric poems... In accordance with the spirit of Greek mythology, the gods themselves stand at the head of this succession of poets, namely, Hermes, the inventor of the lyre, and Apollo, who received the invention from his brother, and became the divinity presiding over the whole art of music (1876: 59).

> Lastly, as the son of the Muse Calliope (Καλλιόπη), meaning "beautiful voice," Orpheus is said to have

lived in Thrace at the period of the Argonauts, whom he accompanied in their expedition. Presented with the lyre [herein "stringed-instrument"] by Apollo, and instructed by the Muses in its use, he enchanted with its music not only the wild beasts, but the trees and rocks upon Olympus, so that they moved from their places to follow the sound (Ibid: 60-61).

Finally, the name "Orpheus" derives from ὄρφνη meaning "darkness," and, of course, darkness may be variously associated with "the night, the underworld, and death." (cf. Cobb, 1992: 240). Orpheus has a way with words. Orpheus brings meaning to light. Orpheus resonating the dark chaos of material noise with a higher harmony momentarily elucidates a path "ascending" the material dimension. The tragic momentariness, here, is twofold, and it cannot be separated from Orpheus himself. That is, one, as time passes, seasons everything within them change; two, even that which we sustain across change is destined to die. This sustaining requires psychological processes that further estrange us: from what?

70

§2 *Re-currents in the Orpheus Myth*

The Orpheus myth, which we intend here to refer to his Underworld or Deathlands descent in regard to Eurydice, always includes several recurrent themes. First, Orpheus marries Eurydice. Second, Eurydice is bitten by a poisonous serpent – Virgil tells us she was attempting to escape being raped by a "hunter." Third, Eurydice dies. In his new mourning, the music Orpheus composes fills nature with longing and lament. Thus, fourth, Orpheus gains access to and descends into the Underworld or Deathlands. Fifth, an agreement is made involving the King and Queen of the Underworld, i.e. "Hades/Pluto" and "Persephone." According to the agreement, Orpheus may return with Eurydice to life on two conditions. Not all versions of the myth mention both conditions: one, given the unique access to the Underworld granted to Orpheus, he is expressly forbidden from "stealing" any of its secrets; two, Orpheus is not allowed to "turn" or "look backward" to see Eurydice until they have exited the Underworld.

Accepting the terms, Orpheus must ascend from the Underworld with Eurydice following. Yet, per the conditions, he is not allowed to see her ascend. Rather, the "god of traveling," i.e. Hermes, guides her along the path following Orpheus back to life. Of course, Orpheus "turns around" or "looks back," and Eurydice is not restored to life. She returns, guided by Hermes, to the Underworld. Finally, accounts differ in regard to what ultimately happens to Orpheus. That is to say, Orpheus is ultimately killed; however, it is not immediately clear why. We know that he is "torn apart" or "dismembered," reminiscent of the fate of Dionysus. Some accounts make it seem as though his refusal to love another woman leads to his destruction at the hands of angry reveling maenads. Other accounts make it seem as though the "backward glance" of this "Orpheus Moment" is not the only Orphic transgression regarding the Underworld. In other words, perhaps Orpheus was also guilty of "stealing" secrets from the Underworld. This is the aspect of the Myth often referenced as justifying his *sparagmos*. If so, we might ask: how were those secrets passed on to his followers? What are these "secrets," and what difference might knowing them make?

V. Orpheus, Plato, and the Revelation of the Mystery of the *Scala Amoris*

"I once heard one of our sages say that we are now dead,
and the body is our tomb..."

~Plato

(*Gorgias*, 493a).

§1 *A Straightforward Explanation of this Chapter*

Because the next four sections of this chapter deal with ideas that may be difficult for readers to initially encounter, especially without prior exposure to Plato's philosophy, the goal of this section is to characterize the following sections in a more straightforward way.

The goal of this chapter, then, is to place the insights gained from the Orpheus Myth and the above, new, translation of the Rilke poems into the wider context of Platonic philosophy. If we understand the origin and depth of Plato's philosophy, then it makes perfect sense to place these insights into that context; for, Plato's philosophy, more than any other, offers us the proper philosophical context for these insights.

In this way, §2 seeks to state the metaphysics behind the Orpheus myth in the widest possible way. At the outer edges of the Platonic philosophy we find discussions of reincarnation. The philosophical concepts needed to elucidate the Platonic metaphysics here are best referred to by the following two Greek words: *anamnēsis* and *palingenesis*.

Whereas the former term refers to the soul's ability to remember (and, thereby, re-member) across incarnations, the latter term refers to the reality of re-incarnating. Philosophically understanding *palingenesis* is important; however, it is also difficult.

Moreover, these two terms are discussed first, since they provide the widest points from which to contextualize the Mysteries of Orpheus & Eurydice. §3, then, takes Plato's Myth of the Cave (or Cave Allegory) along with his Myth of Er as two points with which to further contextualize the Mysteries of Orpheus & Eurydice. This is, so to speak, a "zooming in" of the context from the discussion of Anamnēsis and Palingenesis. However, all of the points of focus discussed in this chapter may be thought of as if they were stars in a constellation; thus, they continually shine light on the discussion.

The discussion from §3, then, is also carried into §4, as the themes of fate and love function as points of contact between Plato's writings and the Myth of Orpheus. In this way, insights regarding the Eleusinian Mysteries that function in the background of Plato's Myth of the Cave are then connected with Plato's Myth of Er and the Mysteries of Orpheus & Eurydice.

Finally, the connection between Plato's *scala amoris* and the Myth of Orpheus are explicitly elucidated from out of the deeper context already articulated in this chapter. How this differs from the brief characterization in Chapter III, above, is not only that this discussion is more in depth and explicit; rather, it also differs in that it introduces insights from Plato's *Phaedrus* regarding divine mania.

Divine mania (or "divine madness") is involved here in that as we ascend the *scala amoris* into the transcendental dimension, our experience of intensity is heightened. There is some sense in which this is the panic of the lower animal and human (social) levels; however, it is now illuminated from its true point of departure. That is to say, the intensity is awareness of celestial be-ing.

§2 *Palingenesis & Anamnēsis: Persephone's Offer to Orpheus*

Diogenes Laertius (fl. c. 3rd Century AD) memorably referred to Orpheus as "the first philosopher" (1925, Prologue), and Marsilio Ficino (1433-1499 AD) famously provided us with the following genealogy:

Chapter V: The Mystery of the *Scala Amoris*

> In things pertaining to theology there were in former times six great teachers expounding similar doctrines. The first was Zoroaster, the chief of the Magi; the second Hermes Trismegistus, the head of the Egyptian priesthood; Orpheus succeeded Hermes; Aglaophamus was initiated into the sacred mysteries of Orpheus; Pythagoras was initiated into theology by Aglaophamus; and Plato by Pythagoras. Plato summed up the whole of their wisdom... (Ficino, 1559: 698; quoted in Mead, 1896: 18; cf. Kingsley, 1995).

As a result of this genealogy, by the time of Plato, as Patricia Cannon Johnson explained it, "The dividing line between *Nous* and mystical experience is a fine one, and the Hellenistic world was heir to two great modes of contemplation – the Mystery religions and the schools of philosophy of Greece." (Cannon-Johnson, 2010: 143). In this context, then, the Orphic Mysteries, including their involvement in the Mysteries of Dionysus and Eleusis, serve "a double purpose" in that they provide "a Theogony against which to read the philosophic doctrines, and also generates an esoteric language, presenting a key to much within the writings of the Neoplatonists and their successors which may otherwise appear obscure." (Cannon-Johnson, 2010: 144). Of course, this is because both Pythagoras (c. 570 – c. 495 BC) and Plato (428/7-348/7 BC) "had been influenced in the development of their ideas by their own experience as initiates of the Mysteries." (Cannon-Johnson, 2010: 144; cf. Ruck 1981; cf. Ruck, 1986; cf. Ruck, 2006).

The "Orphic Mysteries" pertain to the *Orphic Hymns*, i.e. the songs to be sung which reveal the Orphic Theogony and the "Gold Tablets" which instruct initiates regarding future life (Orpheus, 1896). As the purpose here is not an attempt at an exhaustive explication of the *Orphic Hymns*, we suggest – in addition to the primary source – G.R.S. Mead's (1896) book titled *Orpheus*. It is interesting to think of these *Hymns* as Orpheus' revelation of Underworld secrets.

According to Mead, in the Mysteries of Orpheus "the doctrine of reincarnation was fully and scientifically expounded." Just as Plutarch (c. 46 – 120 AD) informed that the story of Dionysus and the Titans is a "sacred narrative concerning reincarnation," so too the Rape of Persephone, "one of the dramatic representations of the [L]esser [M]ysteries," refers to the "descent of souls" in the (re)incarnation process (Mead, 1896: 301). Further, the "presiding deity of rebirth was Hermes" (Ibid: 302). Hence, as this meditation will discuss through Plato's philosophy, the Orpheus myth itself may be understood as pertaining to a doctrine of reincarnation. This doctrine has two primary philosophical components on which we will meditate: *Anamnēsis* and *Palingenesis*.

Re-incarnation, of course, involves being incarnated again. This, in turn, conjures images of cyclic activity and the idea of a wheel. In fact, we are told that this is how Orpheus referred to incarnated life, i.e. as a "Wheel" (Ibid: 300). There are plenty of Underworld images which may be associated with such a Wheel; the primary two discussed in the literature being the "Wheel of Ixion" and Sisyphus' cycles of rock pushing. At times different names may be used such as Pythagoras' "Wheel of Life," "cycles of generation," or "the Wheel of Birth and Re-Birth." What is clear, then, from our Orphic genealogy and the *Orphic Hymns* is that the human soul is *responsible for itself* regarding both the trajectory it occupies in its current cycle of generation, and its "liberation" from the cycling of re-incarnation, i.e. the Wheel. Thus, Orphic philosophy is understood as a practice of liberation, and in this way – as mentioned in previous meditations – regarding the Orphic philosophy, we may discern soteriological, teleological, and even eschatological aspects.

Perhaps astonishing when we first discover the fact, Plato believed the practice of philosophy is properly "the practice of dying" (Plato 1997g: 64a5-6 & 67d7-10). Of course, the Platonic context for this insight is that the body is a kind of "tomb" or "prison" for the soul or psychē (cf. Plato 1997a; b; c; f; g; i; & j).

Chapter V: The Mystery of the *Scala Amoris*

Three questions seem to immediately follow: (1) Why is the soul imprisoned? (2) Can the soul be liberated from the imprisonment that is its embodiment? (3) What is the relationship between the soul's embodied-imprisoned be-ing and its be-ing when non-embodied? These questions will be answered by the end of this (long) section.

Of course, the first question involves the various "descent" portions of myths regarding the Underworld, i.e. the Deathlands. In the case of Persephone, lust and rape precipitate descent, and in the case of Orpheus it is love. The second question opens onto a Platonic psychology, an account of psychē, which – before it begins to fully address the third question – must provide some insight into the nature of the soul that allows for its liberation.

Finally, once we are primed to meditate on the third question, we may wonder about the difference between embodied and celestial temporality. That is to say, if the experience of our life, i.e. if the experience of the passing of time, depends on our embodiment, then the embodied experience of time is part of be-ing entombed or imprisoned. What would that which we call "time" while embodied be, when the soul is no longer imprisoned?

Toward developing a response to these questions consider the following quote from the Neoplatonist Porphyry (c. 234-c. 305 AD), the student responsible for publishing the writings of his teacher Plotinus (204/5- 270 AD), i.e. the *Enneads*.

> That which nature binds, nature also dissolves: and that which the soul binds, the soul likewise dissolves. Nature, indeed, bound the body to the soul, but the soul binds herself to the body. Nature, therefore, liberates the body from the soul; but the soul liberates herself from the body. ... Hence, there is a two-fold death; the one, indeed, universally known, in which the body is liberated from the soul; but the other peculiar to Philosophers [initiates], in which the soul is liberated from the body. (quoted in Mead, 1896).

77

Thus, the question we may now ask is: How does soul remain gripped to its body? Answering this question goes far toward answering both of the first two questions asked above regarding psychē's imprisonment.

Before turning to Plato's dialogs, consider the following toward developing the Platonic philosophy as Orphic in origin. On the one hand, as the activity of thinking properly belongs to psychē, not body, devotion to the proper principle of thought, which is truth, contributes to psychē's liberation from the Wheel of (re)incarnation, and this insight will invoke Plato's notion of *anamnēsis*. On the other hand, notice the insight to be pursued by thinking into our three-question-complex problem from the "celestial" point of view. That is to say, is this (here and now) psychē's first time "around" the Wheel (cf. Scalambrino, 2015c)? The insight gained from, even just simply asking, this question invokes the philosophical notion of *palingenesis* through *anamnēsis*.

In Plato's dialog *Cratylus*, we listen in as Socrates provides etymological explanation of the terms for "body" and "soul." The following statements are all made by Socrates

> When you consider the nature of every body, what, besides the soul, do you think sustains and supports it, so that it lives and moves about? ... So, a fine name to give this power, which supports and sustains the whole of nature (*physis*/φύσις), would be 'nature-sustainer' (*phusechē*). This may be pronounced more elegantly, '*psuchē*' [i.e. *psychē*/ψυχή]. (Plato, 1997c: 400a-c).

Next, in regard to the body Socrates explains,

> some people say that the body (*sōma*) is the tomb (*sēma*) of the soul, on the grounds that it is entombed in its present life while others say that it is correctly called 'a sign' ('*sēma*') because the soul signifies whatever it wants to signify by means of the body. *I think it is the followers of Orpheus who gave the body*

78

> *its name* [emphasis added], with the idea that the soul
> is being punished for something, and that the body is
> an enclosure or prision in which the soul is securely
> kept – as the name '*sōma*' itself suggests – until the
> penalty is paid... (Plato, 1997c: 400c-d).

Here Plato explicitly connects the understanding of body as prison or
tomb with Orpheus. Of course, this is the same understanding upon
which the *Phaedo* determines that proper practice of philosophy is the
practice of dying.

Further, notice in regard to the question of the soul's descent
into the body, in the *Meno* Plato explicitly references the Persephone-
Demeter myth. Moreover, Plato at the key point of the dialog – just
before the famous "Pythagorean Theorem" passage – introduces
anamnēsis in the very context of the soul's immortality, noting:

> I know what you want to say, Meno. Do you realize
> what a debater's argument you are bringing up, that a
> man cannot search either for what he knows or for
> what he does not know? He cannot search for what he
> knows – since he knows it, there is no need to search –
> nor for what he does not know, for he does not know
> what to look for. (Plato, 1997f: 80e-81).

The idea here is that we are presented with a perplexity the resolution
of which reveals the notion of *anamnēsis*. That is to say, learning is
re-collecting [*anamnēsis*] through the psychic dimension, as if "out"
of the body.

Quoting a poem from Pindar (fr. 133), Socrates goes on –
after what to my ears sounds like a reference to both the Eleusinian
Mysteries and Orpheus – to explain,

> They say that the human soul is immortal; at times it
> comes to an end, which they call dying; at times it is
> reborn, but it is never destroyed, and one must
> therefore live one's life as piously as possible [quoting
> Pindar]:

> Persephone will return to the sun above in the ninth year
> the souls of those from whom
> she will exact punishment for old miseries,
> and from these come noble kings,
> mighty in strength and greatest in wisdom,
> and for the rest of time men will call them sacred heroes.

> As the soul is immortal, has been born often, and has
> seen all things here and in the underworld, there is
> nothing which it has not learned; so it is in no way
> surprising that it can recollect the things it knew
> before... (Plato, 1997f: 81b-d; cf. Plato, 1997g: 72c5-6).

Of all on which we may meditate, consider just the following: Plato here links the immortality of the soul with descent into the Underworld; *anamnēsis* with liberation and in connection with the Queen of the Deathlands Persephone; and, he indicates a "sacred" hierarchy along the trajectory of liberation from the Wheel of (re)incarnation, i.e. "sacred heroes" (more on this below).

Thus, keeping in mind that Socrates in the *Cratylus* brought the focus of the question to our "present life," we are reminded both of the earlier question: Is this our first time "around"? And, the third question of our three-question-complex problem, viz. "Where" are we in the hierarchy of liberation? As one commentator aptly put it, with such an understanding of embodiment,

> The question shifted from that of one's status among
> the dead, in an afterlife that was real in the same way
> as successive cycles of Eternal Return, to that of
> whether one had awakened, in *this* life, to a
> transcending spiritual and interior life that knows its
> own eternity already and in death is released from the
> cycle of birth and death and from worldly existence
> altogether (Manchester, 1986: 392).

Just as Grace may be understood as a gift from God, the revelation of the "path" leading to psychē's liberation may be understood as a "gift from the gods to men" (Plato, 1997i: 16c; cf. Plato, 1997g: 66b), and, in this way, of the Orphic understanding of the soul's liberation from the Wheel of (re)incarnation it may be said that "Plato took over from Orphics or Pythagoreans, a doctrine of sin, purgatory, reincarnation, and eventual purification" (Bostock, 2000: 893; cf. Mead, 1896: 300).

Now, the idea here is ultimately that humans are re-incarnated, and depending upon how one lives life determines the next incarnation. The perplexity with which I have been grappling since becoming a "Doctor of Philosophy" may be articulated as zeroing in on the "frequency assumption" of (re)incarnation. In other words, I understand be-ing to dynamically be the condition for the possibility of one's psychic incarnation. In this way, the "frequency rate" of (re)incarnation refers to the continual pulsing of the human psychē's be-ing in embodied time.

We can approach this thought differently. Humans are capable of an experience of time-dilation, e.g. try *zazen*. I take this to be a glimpse of embodied time from the celestial point of view. *Psychē* loosens its grip on *physis*. Beyond the clearly discernible theoretical conclusion, merely from meditating on the above paragraph's content, a tendency toward the deconstruction of (worldly) identity follows from the actual experience of time-dilation. In a Jungian vocabulary time-dilation is a descent through the Shadow of Persona in psychē's re-turn to Self. Put more bluntly and Platonically, your identity is the result of a "Shadow Game." *If psychē is in a process of (re)incarnation, then your self-understanding, insofar as it is in terms of embodiment and the social, would be psychē's mud-marking for solely this time around the Wheel.* Keep in mind, this is a metaphysical conclusion, this is not an ethical practical recommendation (as if illusory identity means all is permissible; quite the contrary, according to Orpheus).

Suddenly, it is as if the "momentariness" of embodied existence shines forth in that psychē's grip on *physis* is temporal. Our be-ing "pulses," then, as through this "death" the "soul is liberated from the body" (think of the second block-quote of this section). *This is palingenesis*. That is to say, whether we understand the re-incarnation as a pulsing of psychē into *physis* at the moment of the body's total birth and death (this would be from the perspective of the body) or we understand the re-incarnation as a pulsing of psychē into *physis* in the im-prison-ing process keeping psychē from liberation from this body (this would be from the perspective of the psychē), in both cases the – what I call – "pulsing" refers to psychē's be-ing embodied; the idea of which is called *"palingenesis"* (cf. Scalambrino, 2011).

The ideas of *anamnēsis* and *palingenesis* come together in Plato's *Phaedo*, aka *On the Soul*. Just as through *anamnēsis* the soul communes with the higher invisible dimensions of (i.e. conditioning) human reality, so too for heuristic purposes this may be understood as the realm of the "Platonic Forms." Of course, these Forms are "deathless and indestructible." Thus we hear Socrates ask, "Do we say that there is such a thing as the Just itself, or not? ... And the Beautiful, and the Good?" (Plato, 1997g: 65d). The philosophers answer, "Of course." Socrates then asks, "have you ever seen any of these things with your eyes? ... Or have you ever grasped them with any of your *bodily* [emphasis added] senses?" (Plato, 1997g: 65d). Of course, we have not.

With this Socrates explains that the extent to which one can "approach" these beings without influence from the body is the extent to which one may relate to them as they *truly* are, i.e. in their true be-ing. Truth here is in terms of *alētheia*, i.e. the revelation of these beings. Notice we may think of a spectrum here in terms of privation of the material dimension, and insofar as the bodily material dimension obscures psychē's en-visioning of these beings, then less material bodily influence means more revelation of these higher beings. The spectrum, for psychē, is as if from the carnal to the celestial. Socrates explains, "he will do this most perfectly who approaches... with thought alone, without ... dragging in any sense perception..." (Plato, 1997g: 66a).

Socrates culminates this discussion by communicating what "All these things will necessarily make the true philosophers believe and say to each other" (Plato, 1997g: 66b). Given its importance, we quote him at length:

> There is likely to be something such as a path to guide us out of our confusion, because as long as we have a body and our soul is fused with such an evil we shall never adequately attain what we desire, which we affirm to be the truth. The body keeps us busy in a thousand ways because of its need for nurture. Moreover, if certain diseases befall it, they impede our search for the truth. It fills us with wants, desires, fears, all sorts of illusions and much nonsense, so that, as it is said, in truth and in fact no thought of any kind ever comes to us from the body. Only the body and its desires cause war, civil discord and battles, for all wars are due to the desire to acquire wealth, and it is the body and the care of it, to which we are enslaved, which compel us to acquire wealth, and all this makes us too busy to practice philosophy.
>
> ...
>
> *It really has been shown to us* that, if we are ever to have pure knowledge, *we must escape from the body* and observe things in themselves *with the soul by itself*. It seems likely that *we shall, only* then, *when we are dead, attain that* which we desire and *of which we claim to be lovers* ... after death. Then and not before, the soul is apart from the body [all emphases added].
> (Plato, 1997g: 66b-67a).

This sounds like what Orpheus must have thought prior to entering the Deathlands to retrieve Eurydice. To attain what we love, we must die, and thereby Plato justifies directing our love away from *this life* and the body (cf. Luke 9:24).

Before following out the meditation on love which Socrates begins for us, let us conclude this portion of our meditation regarding *anamnēsis* and *palingenesis*. Recalling the Forms, Socrates explains "the Beautiul and the Good and all *that kind* [emphasis added] of reality ... just as they exist, so our soul must exist before we are born." (Plato, 1997g: 76e). Further, "All would agree ... that the god, and the Form of life itself and anything that is deathless, are never destroyed." (Plato, 1997g: 106d). Hence, Socrates concludes in Plato's dialog *Phaedo* (On the Soul), "the soul ... is most certainly deathless and indestructible and our souls ... really dwell in the underworld." (Plato, 1997g: 107a).

Explaining what such an after-embodied-life experience will be like, Socrates explains he is basing his comments on "the sacred rites," and we are to understand Socrates (and Plato) are referencing (their) initiation into the Eleusinian Mysteries. According to Socrates, "after being judged" souls "proceed to the underworld," yet,

> the soul that is passionately attached to the body, as I said before, hovers around it and the visible world for a long time, struggling and suffering much until it is led away by force and with difficulty by its appointed spirit ... the soul that has led a pure and moderate life finds ... gods to guide it (Plato, 1997g: 107e-108c).

Did any part of this passage sound strange to you? Plato has Socrates say that a soul "hovers around ... the visible world"; up to this point in the dialog and these meditations an almost clear cut dualism may have been assumed, i.e. the dead have their place and we have ours. However, this passage shines the light of death on the presence of psychē.

That is to say, psychē is supposed to be (*here and now*) incarnated in a process of (re)incarnation, i.e. falling along the turning Wheel. What is more, recall from this meditation's epigraph – yet to be fully discussed – that from the celestial point of view, it is as if embodiment is death. Do you suppose Orpheus went about asking passersby "How do you get to the Deathlands?" From the Orphic-

Platonic insights that the soul does not die and that embodiment is death, we may understand en-trance into the Deathlands as a kind of psychic relationality. For example, what would an after-embodied-life experience be like in terms of a celestial point of view regarding *palingenesis*?

The very memory ladder which allows for a time-dilation in which psychē may experience more "by itself," "away from – despite – the body," or from a "celestial point of view," is the very memory that haunts *this* body.

Rhythmically, weaving along the pulse of celestial music, this memory simultaneously grips and writes the moment at a focal point of love. Yet, just as the term "simultaneous" may seem problematic to us there must be a "delay" or "time lag" given the frequency at which *physis* is becoming, i.e. over-flowing-ly keeping psychē bound in its current configuration. Thus a "filled time duration" illusion veils the becoming-tomb continuously be-ing constructed "around" psychē. Through time-dilation and "true philosophy" glimpsing "under" this veil, i.e. en-trance into embodied experience as the Deathlands, is possible.

As we have heard in this section, then, when – what Plato calls – a "true philosopher" follows the path of *anamnēsis* toward "purification" and "away from" embodiment, this path leads to liberation. The truth of liberation revealed along this path resounds the celestial point of view regarding the Wheel of (re)incarnation, *palingenesis*, and en-trance into the Deathlands through awareness of embodiment as psychē's tomb. We juxtapose these insights with a commentator's reminder,

> Orpheus is primarily associated with the magic influence of his lyre, whose notes enchanted the wild beasts... he was also an inspired theologian who discovered and revealed the way to Immortality and exhorted men "to escape from death." The music of Orpheus' lyre enchanted even the implacable lord of Hades. (Bikerman, 1939: 368; cf. Alceus, fr. 80).

The "escape from death" involves enchanting those guardians of the Deathlands. We sing the song our soul can re-member – *anamnēsis* – from the pure song of Orpheus. Recall from the Rilke poem, translated above, from the lyre of Orpheus "more lament came than ever from lamenting women," such "that a world of lament was made." This world of lament ... the souls who sing its truth to Persephone, "*for the rest of time* [emphasis added] men will call them sacred heroes" (Plato, 1997f: 81b-d).

§3 *Plato's Cave: The Eleusinian Mysteries & Orpheus*

As we, of course, all know well by now, the "Cave Allegory" begins by describing the "*prisoners*" chained in the cave. The Allegory begins with *Republic* Book VII (514a2) and is usually said to extend to 519c5. Recall, further, that Socrates initiates the Cave Allegory with the following statement: "compare the effect of education and the lack of it on our nature to an experience like this" (Plato, 1997k: 541a1). As we have already seen from the above discussion regarding *Meno* and *Phaedo*, learning is *anamnēsis*. Hence, the Cave Allegory should be sounding more and more like a reference to the "Sacred Mysteries" of Orpheus.

Plato notoriously never explicitly states two points regarding the Cave Allegory which are of great importance for both memorizing the narrative and the journey it describes. First, Plato never tells us how or why a "prisoner" is able to escape the chains binding them to the shadowy dimension of the Cave. Second, Plato never tells us why a liberated prisoner who had seen outside the Cave would return. On the one hand, we may understand the openness of the narrative regarding both of these aspects to suggest the need for myth. On the other hand, the Wheel of (re)incarnation would explain, at least, the possibility of the prisoners "leaving" and "re-turning" to the Cave. Moreover, it is possible to understand this movement out and in to the Cave in terms of *palingenesis*.

In language, then, that is clearly reminiscent of the *Meno* and *Phaedo* discussions of *anamnēsis*, Plato has Socrates explain,

the power to learn is present in everyone's soul and
that the instrument with which each learns *is like an
eye* [emphasis added] that cannot be turned around
from darkness to light without turning the whole body.
This instrument cannot be turned around from that
which is coming into being [i.e. Becoming] without
turning the whole soul (Plato, 1997k: 518c-d).

He concludes *anamnēsis* is precisely the process of turn-ing that
which "is like an eye" in psychē "upward." That this refers to
developing a "philosophical" life is clear in that the soul's turn-ing
depends on "habit and practice." It should not be surprising then that,
for example, it is possible to read Joseph Campbell's *The Hero with a
Thousand Faces* as a discussion of this movement up along the
hierarchy of psyche's ascent (Campbell, 2008).

Of course, multiple factors influence the movement
"upward" and "out" of the Cave. In what some may understand in
terms of "karma," thinking of *palingenesis*, the soul must contend
with the accumulated "momentum" of its past (lives). It must also
develop through "habit and practice" the ability to orient itself
appropriately in its present (life). This orientation culminates in a
circumspect attitude toward the future.

The "practice" we understand to be the "practice of dying"
discussed in the *Phaedo*. Thus, combining two pieces here (from
Phaedo and *Republic*) the prohibition against playing "Shadow
Games" belongs in the context of psychē's liberation from the
Cave/flesh-tomb. Regarding the use of that which "is like an eye" in
psychē, Socrates explains that if one who had seen the truth of
psychē's embodiment "had to compete again with the perpetual
prisoners in recognizing the shadows, wouldn't he invite ridicule?
Wouldn't it be said of him that he'd returned from his upward journey
with his eyesight ruined [?]" (Plato, 1997k: 517a).

What we see, then, is that there is an analogy of hierarchy
between what is above and what is below. The competition among
"perpetual prisoners" regarding the shadows results in a hierarchy

among those who desire – ultimately – *more* Cave-dwelling, i.e. an Underworld throne. Likewise, we may also speak of a hierarchy regarding stages of development toward "final nirvana" (cf. Scalambrino, 2012; cf. Scalambrino 2015c) or liberation from the Wheel of (re)incarnation. However, the difference between psychē's relation to the material dimension of Becoming and psychē's relation to its own trajectory of liberation – if we must speak in terms of logical binaries – are opposites. That is to say, the requirement of "gaining ideas" for advancement in the Shadow dimension hinders psychē's "advancement" regarding liberation (cf. Suzuki, 2011: 25).

There are two points left to discuss before moving to the next part of this meditation. First, the manner in which Plato provides references to Orpheus in the *Phaedo* which we will read in the context of the Cave Allegory, i.e. specifically the "Shadow Games." Second, the symbolism of hierarchy regarding psychē's liberation as it resounds throughout Plato's *Republic* and especially his Book X "Myth of Er" discussion, which also includes reference to Orpheus.

First, notice the large lacuna between believing in an after-life and believing that this life *is death* for the soul. Beyond Socrates' use of the "lyre" and the "mute swan" as examples, Socrates says something quite enigmatic (77d4-78b4) regarding how a philosopher should respond to someone who believes in – what I fondly call – the "Poof All Gone" theory of the soul, i.e. the belief held by many "Modern" psychologists that whatever it is to which "soul" refers it is simply annihilated at the death of the body.

Socrates tells us, "You seem to have an immature fear that the wind would really dissolve and scatter the soul, as it leaves the body, especially if one happens to die in a high wind and not in calm weather." (Plato, 1997g: 77e). His interlocutors, of course, find his manner of putting it humorous. Yet, they press him to actually tell them how they should respond to someone who has such an "immature fear," and here is the enigmatic response they receive: "You should sing a charm over him every day until you have charmed away his fears." (Plato, 1997g: 77e7). On the one hand, Socrates seems to see the "Poof All Gone" belief as if in terms of psychē's courage. On the other hand, the "singing" of a "charm" should be understood as a reference to Orpheus.

Thus, it is as if the "prisoners" playing Shadow Games fear death, because the motor force of the Shadow Games is characterized by avarice or acquisitiveness or covetousness; so, death indicates for the prisoners the inability to gain more, i.e. to acquire and consume more. The singing of charms, as will be discussed in just a moment is supposed to function as a kind of "catharsis." In regard to the ancient uses of this term we hear,

> metaphorically, *katharsis* presents seven pictures. (1) In one ancient papyrus *katharsis* is 'clearing,' as when a person is clearing the land of twigs and stones. (2) In another papyrus *katharsis* is 'winnowing,' as in the thrashing of grain. (3) Diocles used the term as the image of 'cleaning' when he described the process of cleaning food by cooking it. (4) Theophrastus, in his essay 'On Plants,' meant 'pruning' when he used *katharsis* in relation to trees. (5) Both Philodemus ... and Epicurus ... used the same word to picture the 'clarification' achieved by explanation. (6) Galen, of course, used *katharsis* to signify the 'healing' of an illness by the application of medicine. And (7) Chrysippus' *katharsis* was the 'purifying' of the universe by fire. (Miller, 1970: 44; cf. Aristotle, 1995: 1449b; cf. Lucas, 1977).

Thus, psychē's purification brings clarification in terms of human experience and the Deathlands, prepares psychē for Judgment at the cessation of the body's existence in this life, and from the celestial point of view leads to harmony and psychē's becoming more whole as a celestial be-ing.

Further, for Plato, hearing these charms/learning these Orphic truths (*anamnēsis*) is involved in the process of Orphic purification (*palingenesis*) in relation to embodiment and the Wheel of (re)incarnation, which may be understood in Eastern terms of "enlightenment" and "nirvana" or in Western terms such as "conversion" and "Heaven." In this way, like the archetypal Phoenix, "the Orphic cosmos, child of Night and rising out of Chaos, becomes the fundamental topos of the cave." (McGahey, 1994: 49). Any true dynamics of psychē must account for the possibility of such a *transformation*. Thus, Jung criticized Freud's inability to think through "conversion." According to Jung, "Freud founders on the question of Nicodemus: 'How can a man be born when he is old? Can he enter the second time into his mother's womb, and be born?'" (Jung, 1961a: 340; cf. John 3:4). Moreover, in a statement which will take on even more meaning in the next section of this meditation, Socrates refers to the hearing of such charms suggesting "there is nothing on which you could spend your money to a greater advantage." (Plato, 1997g: 78a6; cf. Schindler, 2009).

Just as Plato – throughout his dialogs – divides the various possible ways of directing psychē in terms of the love of money, honor, or wisdom, so too it is the love of wisdom that leads to purification and liberation. This division of "kinds of lovers" coincides with the *scala amoris* of the *Symposium* for the very reason that they both characterize psychē's ascension of its Deathland's flesh-tomb. As the discussion of the second and concluding point of this section of the meditation will examine, another hierarchy, this time from the *Republic*, may also be understood in terms of psychē's ascent.

In his excellent 1903 article titled "Plato and Orpheus," Francis M. Cornford set out to "trace in the mythical setting of some of the Platonic dialogs certain religious conceptions which Plato borrowed from Orphism, and to show how he transformed them to his own philosophical uses." (Cornford, 1903: 433). Ultimately Cornford concludes,

> It is plain, I think, that in the Cave-myth the ceremonies of initiation are in Plato's mind and suggest the imagery ... We are to understand that education in the highest sense is an initiation; it

involves deliverance from the prison of the senses, a
vision purified to apprehend truth, a death into life, an
exaltation of man's spirit to unity with the divine. (Ibid:
439).

Note that the language of "unity" should also call to mind Jung's
discussion of the *mysterium coniunctionis*.

Further, according to Cornford, "To the Orphic it is by
purification that the deliverance from the bodily tomb is
accomplished. [Analogous to the distinction between "Nirvana" and
"Final Nirvana."] Ceremonial purification preceded the initiatory rite:
physical death was a fuller purification from the muddy vesture of
decay." (Ibid: 437). Quoting the Neoplatonist Proclus, then, he points
to an interpretation which suggests Plato meant "to divide all rational
natures into four: (1) gods, (2) spirits, (3) heroes, (4) men" (Cornford,
1903: 434). Cornford later tells us Plato refers to the fourth division
as "husbandmen and craftsmen" (Ibid: 435).

Cornford provides a translation of what he refers to as "the
Pythagorean" description of "preliminary purification" found in the
records of Iamblicus:

it will be well to consider what a great length of time
we have spent in scouring away the stains that were
deeply engrained in our breasts, until at last as the
years went by, we became able to receive the master's
words. (Cornford, 1903: 437; cf. Iamblicus, 1918: 40).

On the one hand, this Pythagorean characterization of *palingenesis*
clearly includes an understanding of *this life*, i.e. this current
embodiment, as a moment along the trajectory of psychē's ascent. On
the other hand, though the author of the above "Pythagorean"
description may have had Pythagoras in mind with the word
"master," it seems appropriate that he may just as well have had
Orpheus in mind.

As an illustration of the thought, Cornford engages in a
meditation on the etymological explication of "Apollo" which Plato has
Socrates perform in *Cratylus*. There we find "four functions" derived

from the name "Apollo," and the notion of the "Sun-God" is operable here for its connection to ascension toward the Sun and out of the Cave. These four functions are "music, divination, medicine, archery." (Cornford, 1903: 437). Cornford reminds us that "Music is derived from "μῶσθαι and means *search* and *philosophy*." (Ibid: 438).

Finally, there are three kinds of purification: (1) physical – and this involves drugs; (2) purification of the soul – this involves purifying ceremonies and the singing of "charms," i.e. hymns; (3) purification by enthusiasm – and this involves exaltation. Moreover, the latter two may involve exhortation, and, beyond being Son of Apollo and synthesizer of Apollo and Dionysus, of course, Orpheus was "Famous for his charms and incantations [(*epodai* and *pharmaka*)]" (Uždavinys, 2011: 38; cf. Entralgo, 1970).

Notice, regarding this "purification by enthusiasm," that the term "enthusiasm" comes from the Greek ἐνθουσιασμός, which may be analyzed into: ἐν, θεός, and ουσία, which – respectively – mean "possession," "God," and "substance" or "essence." Hence, to be enthusiastic is to be filled with the substance of the gods. Cornford suggests, rightly I believe, that the Cave Allegory depicts a catharsis and purification such that the "loosening" of a prisoner's chains corresponds to the purification and healing which conditions ascension – ascending the *scala amoris*. Thus, *our incarnations stand in the balance, regarding Persephone's offer to Orpheus. The lament world of Orpheus allows him to glance at her one more time, while re-incarnation after re-incarnation pays for Persephone's grief.*

Finally, we conclude this section of the meditation by discussing the "picking of a life" theme from the Myth of Er toward a conclusion of this meditation which combines the following thoughts: (1) Plato's division of "rational natures"; (2) the Cave Allegory as depicting psychē's imprisonment and symbolically representing her potential ascension; (3) the *Meno*'s mention of Persephone regarding *anamnēsis*; (4) the Pythagorean understanding of this current embodiment in the context of *palingenesis*.

Chapter V: The Mystery of the *Scala Amoris*

Recall, the Myth of Er involves Socrates' retelling of Er's narrative from his – what today we might call – "near death" experience. That is, Er died and went to a "pasture" where he was allowed to witness the process by which the gods judge souls and through which souls are re-incarnated. This pastoral vista, of course, included the infamous river Lethē. In addition to Lethē as one of the five (5) bodies of water in the Underworld, i.e. Acheron, Cocytus, Phlegethon, and Styx (the effects of some of these rivers are characterized in terms of hypnosis and trance-like dwelling), we are told of a "well of Memory." This water is mentioned in the Orphic Gold Tablets, as those initiated in the Mysteries of Orpheus are explicitly instructed to drink from the water of Memory. Some commentators refer to the well of Memory as a river or lake.

Er's account is consistent with the idea that as souls pass through this transitional phase in the process of *palingenesis* they are instructed upon receiving their judgment to drink from the river of forgetfulness, i.e. Lethē, so that upon their re-incarnation, they will neither remember their judgment nor their past embodiments; though both still influence their subsequent incarnation. There is also, in the Myth of Er, another key component determining a soul's subsequent incarnation. It involves "the Fates."

According to Er, "your daimon, or guardian spirit will not be assigned to you by lot; you must choose him." (Plato, 1997k: 617d7). Basically, in what amounts to a kind of lottery for picking from the available lives and features of lives, souls choose a daimon, then a "model" of a life, and "all the other things were there, mixed with each other and with wealth, poverty, sickness, health, and the states intermediate to them." (Ibid: 618b3). Thus, certain events and features of each of psychē's embodiments are understood to be "fated."

In this way, we may understand *palingenesis* as involving the progress across multiple lives, or embodiments, while also understanding the possibility of an oscillating progress toward ultimate liberation from the Wheel of (re)incarnation. In this vein, Plato explains that

> if someone pursues philosophy in a sound manner when he comes to live here on earth and if the lottery doesn't make him one of the last to choose, then, given what Er has reported about the next world, it looks as though not only will he be happy here, but his journey from here to there and back again won't be along the rough underground path, but along the smooth heavenly one. (Plato, 1997: 619e)

In the context of this explanation, Orpheus is mentioned. We hear that Er "said that he saw the soul that had once belonged to Orpheus choosing a swan's life, because he hated the female sex because of his death at their hands, and so was unwilling to have a woman conceive and give birth to him." (Plato, 1997k: 620a4). Whatever we make of the misogyny reportedly associated with Orpheus, the association with the swan is a clear link with Phaedo 84e4, and in terms of *palingenesis* it conjures the idea of Orpheus' final re-birth and "Swan Song," and the idea that the very song of Orpheus is the soteriological Swan Song of which its understanding (*anamnēsis*) is wedded to progression on the Orphic path (*palingenesis*) to liberation.

§4 *From the Eternal Nature of Yearning to Henosis: Fate, Destiny, and Love*

The above section left us with a puzzle regarding Plato's idea of philosophy as the "practice of dying." and its relation to Orpheus. It involves the idea of choosing a "daimon" and the relation between a "guardian spirit" and psychē. Further, recall how, quoting Proclus, Cornford pointed to an interpretation suggesting Plato meant "to divide all rational natures into four: (1) gods, (2) spirits, (3) heroes, (4) men" (Cornford, 1903: 434). Couple this with the following from Plato's *Cratylus* (which Cornford himself references), "I agree that every man who is good is of a spiritual nature (δαιμόνιος), whether living or dead, and is rightly called a spirit." (Plato, 1997b: 397b).

The ancient idea which resolves this puzzle we should note well. Cornford, in discussing various references to the Mysteries by ancient Greek playwrights, notes, "The Chorus of initiates in the *Cretans* of Euripides claim that *they have become one with their god* ... The initiate who has reached ὁσίωσις [*hosiosis, i.e. the hierosgamos of henosis*], the supreme consecration *is* a bacchos: the god has entered into him." (Cornford, 1903: 441). Moreover, the Platonic term that captures the meaning of Euripides' *hosiosis* is *henosis*.

Hence, the puzzle is resolved by realizing that regarding some phase of *palingenesis* it is as if psychē merges (henosis) with – think *mysterium coniunctionis* – the daimon (δαιμόνιος) woven to it by fate (cf. *2nd Series, Sonnet 21*). Thus, Cornford can say,

> the souls, by nature and divine justice, rise from men
> to heroes, and from heroes to spirits, and at last, if as
> in the mysteries they be perfectly cleansed and
> consecrated ... then they attain the fairest and final
> bliss and ascend from spirits to gods. (1903: 442).

We understand this final phase of ascension to be beatitude; a state discussed at length by Plato in *Phaedrus*. This notion is also relevant to the previous meditation's discussion of the "restoration of a relation with the gods." We will meditate further on this in the next section of this meditation. Suffice to say at this point, it seems an ancient Greek understanding would allow that one who has a daimon may eventually *be* the daimon.

Now, recalling that humans have free will, despite fated aspects of each embodied existence, we may make a distinction between fate and destiny (cf. Heidegger, 2008). As such, pointing to the sense in which destiny involves a destination which may or may not be reached, may be arrived at in various ways, and finally involves some degree of choice from the traveler, destiny seems more appropriate for the aspects of life more under the individual's control than those aspects which were fated.

It is as if to become incarnated is to take on what the Sacred Mysteries understood as the eternal yearning of (*physis*) material nature (cf. Schelling, 2019). By way of Orphic suffering, that yearning can be transformed into love. From another point of view, this is psychē's trajectory toward *henosis* in the celestial dimension. In other words, it is a spiritual ascending into a new relation toward reality and the increase of a lower, to a higher, power.

I suggest we disagree with Maurice Blanchot's characterization of Orpheus as "careless" and "unconcerned" (though I recognize Blanchot's need to characterize Orpheus as such for the sake of his work in regard to "writing"); yet, I affirm that his characterization of Orpheus in terms of freedom seems philosophically correct. As Blanchot aptly noted,

> Orpheus' gaze is the extreme moment of freedom, the
> moment in which he frees himself of himself and …
> frees the sacred contained in the work, *gives* the sacred
> to itself, to the freedom of its essence which is freedom.
> (Blanchot, 1981: 104).

Spiritually speaking, what you love determines who you are. As mentioned above, Plato's three kinds of lovers are divided into the love of money, the love of honor, and the love of wisdom. Thus, the Wheel of Fortune is also associated with the Wheel of (re)incarnation. Of course, in the context of a meditation on Orpheus, what about Eros? What about love between humans?

Interestingly just as there are multiple ancient Greek terms for love (cf. Lewis, 1971), so too Plato associates psychē's ascension with a development of love. In this way, Plato positions avarice and bodily desires closer to the mud, i.e. the types of relations between psychē and *physis* which pull psychē "down" and away from liberation from the Wheel of (re)incarnation (cf. 1 Timothy 6:10).

Plato provides the explicit connection for which we are looking in the following passages from *Gorgias* and *Timaeus*. To begin, we hear "I shouldn't be surprised that Euripides' lines are true when he says:

> But who knows whether being alive is being dead
> And being dead is being alive?" (Plato, 1997c: 492d).

This statement initiates another etymological analysis revealing Plato's deep affinity with Orphic views.

> Perhaps in reality we're dead. Once I even heard one of the wise men say that we are now dead and that our bodies are our tombs, and that the part of our souls in which our appetites reside is actually the sort of thing to be open to persuasion and to shift back and forth. And hence some clever man, a teller of stories, a Sicilian, perhaps, or an Italian, named this part a jar [*pithos*], on account of its being a persuadable [*pithanon*] and suggestible thing, thus slightly changing the name. And fools [*anoētoi*] he named uninitiated [*amuētoi*], suggesting that that part of the souls of fools where their appetites are located is their undisciplined part, one not tightly closed, a leaking jar, as it were. He based the image on its insatiability. (Plato, 1997c: 493a1-b4).

Socrates goes on to explain that this Italian or Sicilian man

> shows that of the people in Hades – meaning the unseen [*aïdes*] – these, the uninitiated ones, would be the most miserable. They would carry water into the leaking jar using another leaky thing, a sieve. That's why by the sieve he means the soul... And because they leak, he likened the souls of fools to sieves; for their untrustworthiness and forgetfulness makes them unable to retain anything. (Plato, 1997c: 493b4-c3; cf. Plato, 1997k: 364e; cf. Plato, 1997e: 9.870d-e).

Notice the manner in which Plato's discussion of the uninitiated follows from the lines which he quoted from Euripides above.

These same ideas resound in the *Phaedo* where Socrates explains,

> It is likely that those who established the mystic rites
> for us were no fools, but were speaking in riddles long
> ago when they taught that whoever arrives uninitiated
> in Hades will lie in mud, but the purified and initiated
> will dwell with the gods. (1997g: 69c-d).

Further, just as Euripides emphasizes the ambiguity of life and death in light of the ability to shift between the embodied (terrestrial) and the celestial points of view, so too the embodied fate of the uninitiated transposes onto their fate in Hades. Perhaps, then, the difference is not to be understood in terms of "location," but rather in terms of the extent of each individual's fulfillment of psychē's destiny. This, of course, would be understood in terms, then, of progress regarding *anamnēsis* and *palingenesis*.

The next passages to be examined show Plato "tracing the history of the universe down to the emergence of mankind." (Plato, 1997o: 90e1). They come from *Timaeus* and, thus, provide Plato's explicit discussion of *palingenesis* in terms of embodied sex differences and fate.

> Let us proceed, then, to a discussion of this subject in
> the following way. According to our likely account, all
> male-born humans who lived lives of cowardice or
> injustice were reborn in the second generation as
> women. And this explains why at that time the gods
> fashioned the desire for sexual union, by constructing
> one ensouled living thing in us as well as another one
> in women. This is how they made them in each case.
> There is [in a man] a passage by which fluids exit from
> the body ... From this passage ... [there is] a life-giving
> desire for emission right at the place of venting, and so
> [it] produced the love of procreation. This is why, of
> course, the male genitals are unruly and self-willed,
> like an animal that will not be subject to reason and,

driven crazy by its desires, seeks to overpower everything else. The very same causes operate in women. A woman's womb or uterus, as it is called, is a living thing within her with a desire for childbearing. Now when this remains unfruitful for an unseasonably long period of time, it is extremely frustrated and travels everywhere up and down her body. It blocks up her respiratory passages, and by not allowing her to breathe it throws her into extreme emergencies, and visits all sorts of other illnesses upon her until finally the woman's desire and the man's love bring them together, and ... they sow the seed into the ploughed field of her womb, living things too small to be visible and still without form. ... they nourish these living things so that they can mature inside the womb. Afterwards, they bring them to birth, introducing them to the light of day. (Plato, 1997o: 90e1- 91d6).

In terms of generation, then, we see from the above quote that Plato seems to think a hierarchy of re-incarnation within the human species, in addition to the human species in a hierarchy with other generated beings. Further, he seem to speak of sexual desire from the metaphysical perspective regarding generation as if we are dealing solely with meat machine desires. Regarding these desires, Plato understands resistance to be even more difficult for women than for men, and the judgment to be embodied with a womb, thereby, to be more of a punishment. This too, as we shall discuss, is Orphic in origin. In a moment we will engage in a discussion of generation less dualistically determined.

In the next passage Plato discusses the process of embodiment explicitly in regard to the psychē's being "implanted" into the material bodily dimension of Becoming. Keeping in mind that this is what he is describing illuminates the logical coherency of his discussion of *anamnēsis, palingenesis*, and the attendant punishments and rewards (in terms of Deathland-lived-experiences).

When he had finished this speech, he turned again to the mixing bowl he had used before, the one in which he had blended and mixed the soul of the universe. He began to pour into it what remained of the previous ingredients and to mix them in somewhat the same way ... and assigned each soul to a star. He mounted each soul in a carriage, as it were, and showed it the nature of the universe. ... So, once the souls were of necessity *implanted* in bodies, and these bodies had things coming to them and leaving them, the first innate capacity they would of necessity come to have would be sense perception, which arises out of forceful disturbances. This they all would have. The second would be love, mingled with pleasure and pain. And they would come to have fear and spiritedness as well, plus whatever goes with having these emotions, as well as all their natural opposites. And *if they could master these emotions, their lives would be just*, whereas if they were mastered by them, they would be unjust. And *if a person lived a good life throughout the due course of his time, he would at the end return to his dwelling place in his companion star*, to live a life of happiness that agreed with his character. But if he failed in this, he would be born a second time, now as a woman. And if even then he still could not refrain from wickedness, he would be changed once again, this time into some wild animal that resembled the wicked character he had acquired. And he would have no rest from these toilsome *transformations* until he had dragged that massive accretion of fire-water-air-earth into conformity with the revolution of the Same and uniform within him, and so subdued that turbulent, irrational mass by means of reason. This would *return him to his original condition of excellence*. [emphases added] (Plato, 1997o: 41d-42d).

Thus, despite the chaos of Becoming, i.e. psychic be-ing implanted into a material dimension, psychē recollects (*anamnēsis*) the order from which it originates. Living in accordance with such order, i.e. justice and harmony, aids in the process of *anamnēsis*, and the Orphic belief is that with each successive re-incarnation (however we understand the frequency of such an event) psychē's *palingenesis* may accomplish an ascension to absolute freedom from the Wheel of (re)incarnation.

Of course, this is Destiny, rather than Fate, because the agency of the individual determines the trajectory of *palingenesis*. To illustrate, Plato in the *Phaedrus* tells us, "there is a law of Destiny, that the soul which attains any vision of truth in company with a god is preserved from harm until the next period, and if attaining always is always unharmed." (Plato, 1997h: 248c3-6) According to Guthrie,

> The beginnings of salvation lie within every one of us, since they are identical with the germ of divinity which it is our nature as humans to possess. Yet it does not follow that everyone is assured of a blessed future simply by reason of his origin. By a life of *adikia*, of sinfulness, the divine element may be stifled and the "Titanic nature" in us brought to the surface ... The state of those who have let this happen is far worse than if they had merely been "finished and finite clods, untroubled by a spark." To misuse the divine is to use it to our own damnation. Hence the believer will try to lead the Orphic life ... which aims at the exaltation and purification of our Dionysiac nature in order that we may in the end shake off the last trammels of our earthly selves ... (Guthrie, 1993: 156).

Thus, the question of Eros and authenticity is doubly foolish: first, it fails to truly understand Eros; second, it betrays a preoccupation with the need for validation from others, which is itself merely a double distraction. Try asking a Septuagenarian the following two questions.

Which do you think will find more of a response? (1) Do you think you pursue erotic desires with a sense of authenticity? (2) Are you concerned with what will happen to your soul when you die? (cf. Plato, 1997k: 330d-331b).

In this way, notice the repetition of the ambiguity regarding the place of the Deathlands; there is one pale path unrolling upward like a strip of cotton, and many paths leading to Hell. A downward trajectory occupies the paths that choose Becoming and directs that which is like an eye and the appetites of psychē toward the Wheel of (re)incarnation. Larry Alderink, regarding "The Orphic Life," tells us the "issue of a judgment which divides human beings into two groups with distinct destinies raises a question about the relationship between the sort of life an initiate leads prior to entrance to a reward and the reward itself." (Alderink, 1981: 80). Further,

> The line of demarcation between the two consisted of a judgment; after the judgment there were two destinies, one for souls whose penalty was paid by Persephone's grief and another for souls still tainted by failure to follow an Orphic life. (Alderink, 1981: 88).

Hence, we see again the connection of the Underworld descent of Persephone and Orpheus, the Eleusinian and the Orphic Mysteries, and recalling the *Meno* passage discussed above we now have an explicit connection between the Eleusinian Mysteries, Orpheus, *anamnēsis*, and now *palingenesis* too.

Concluding this section's discussion of "punishment," consider the following from Fernando García Romero.

> Several authors mention another punishment suffered by the Leibethrians [i.e. the women responsible for dismembering Orpheus]. The Leibethrians' behavior toward the mythical singer had regrettable effects on their future reputation either because of the circumstances of his death ... or, as Himerius states, because [these women] were filled with envy when

> they heard Orpheus sing his divine melodies. (de
> Jáuregui, 2011: 340).

In connection with Alderink's discussion above, then, the chthonic
trajectory not only thwarts ascension in terms of *palingenesis* it also
precludes spiritual brilliance and holy *poiesis* (cf. Plato, 1997m: 205b-
c). Per Romero,

> Lesbians attribute their well-known talent for poetry
> and music to the fact that Orpheus' head sailed up from
> the continent to their island across the Aegean Sea ...
> [Yet] the inhabitants of Leibethra were considered to
> have become stupid people with no talent for poetry
> and music as a result of the punishment they received
> from the Gods. (de Jáuregui, 2011: 340).

Thus, this discussion of "punishment" links both with Plato's
discussion just above and the distinction between fate and destiny.
That is to say, whereas it is – according to Plato – a fated aspect of
palingenesis to be entombed in generation with a womb, the destiny
of such beings may also be understood to include more or less
punishment. Whereas the Leibethrian maenads cannot respect the
celestial greatness of Orpheus, the "Lesbians" who find Orpheus'
dismembered head singing still are blessed.

The principle of love in the Orphic-Platonic context traverses
a transformation from *Eros* to *Philia* and *Agápē* (cf. 1 John 4:8; cf.
Lewis, 1971). The image of the "pig" has long been associated with the
chthonically preoccupied, e.g. a jewel pierced pig-snout, the pig who
wants to be eaten, and "don't cast your pearl among swine." From a
Jungian approach to the subject, Marie-Louise von Franz recounts a
"Siberian tale" which points to a real type of feminine nature that can
also be projected as an internal aspect of the male psychē.

> One day a lonely hunter sees a beautiful woman
> emerging from the deep forest on the other side of the
> river. She waves at him and sings ... 'Come, come! My
> nest is near ... He throws off his clothes and swims
> across the river, but suddenly she flies away in the

form of an owl, laughing mockingly at him. When he
tries to swim back to find his clothes he drowns in the
cold water. (Franz, 1964: 187-190).

M-L von Franz suggests the story "symbolizes an unreal dream of
love, happiness, and maternal warmth (her nest) – a dream that lures
men away from reality." (Ibid: 190).

We may see that Orpheus represents a power that – in
depriving maenads the ability to sing – externally symbolizes triumph
over chthonic lures, while internally guarding initiates from "unreal
dreams of love." In terms of the *scala amoris*, this means psychē's
ascension to true philosophy and truth through philosophy. In the
light of non-chthonic love "Reverence awakens a sympathetic power
in the soul, and through this we attract similar qualities in the beings
which surround us, that would otherwise, remain hidden." (Steiner,
1910: 60; cf. Suzuki, 2011: 21; cf. Aristotle, 2009: 1155b16-27 & 1165b1-
12).

Finally, Alderink provides a clarification of the *sōma sēma*
discussion in light of the prohibition against suicide in the *Phaedo*
(59d-69e). As one may rationally discern, if escape from the Wheel of
(re)incarnation is to be desired, then why not commit suicide?
According to Alderink, "the body is a prison, i.e. the *place* where the
soul is guarded. And it is the gods who do the watching; to repeat, that
this is Orphic we have Plato's clear statement." (Alderink, 1981: 64; cf.
Guthrie, 1993: 157).

Thus, the prohibition regarding suicide too derives from the
chthonic nature of the desires required for it to bloom. The traditions
of Orpheus, Plato, and Schopenhauer were aware of this well before
Freud's pseudo-scientific articulation of the thought (cf. Bilsker,
1997).

Recalling the Anaximander quote in the previous meditation,
Alderink notes, "Orphic literature is marked by the effort to give
knowledge ... Knowledge of the distinction between body and soul was
the information which created the distinction between those who can
and those who cannot sustain the judgment the gods pass upon

humans" (Alderink, 1981: 89). What does it mean to "sustain" the judgment? Might this not be reference to the ability to "practice dying," for only the ability to practice dying proves the faithfulness of the participant? The wisdom of the practical circumspection which emerges as this practice develops is a mystery, yet an indication of progression along its trajectory should include *henosis*, i.e. *mysterium coniunctionis* (cf. Suzuki, 2011: 84).

For it is not "escape from the Wheel of (re)incarnation" which we desire as much as *henosis*, i.e. *mysterium coniunctionis*. As Novalis reminds us, "Philosophy is properly Home-sickness..." (cf. Plato, 1997a: 41a).

§5 The *Scala Amoris* to *Divine Madness & Sparagmos: The Scala à la Divine Mania*

Of the volumes that have been written and could still be written on Plato's dialog *Phaedrus*, for our purposes we need to remember that the dialog discusses different kinds of madness, or put more consistent with the Greek, "mania." Plato, unsurprisingly, divides these types of madness in terms of the lower material dimension of Becoming and embodiment and the higher invisible dimension of the soul, the daimonic and God. Thus, as we will meditate on here, Plato speaks of the methodological difference between mechanical technicity and "divine mania." Divine mania, i.e. the higher forms of what is by inhabitants of the lower dimensions seen as madness, accounts for the true philosopher. It is a kind of baptism, if you will, for psychē, an initiation, for which many are – evidently – called, though few are chosen.

Socrates' second speech, sometimes referred to as the "mythical hymn," of the *Phaedrus* (243e-257b) initiates the discussion of divine mania. Even just a glance at the "sub-divisions" of this "hymn" reveals its relation to our mediation regarding philosophy as the practice of dying:

"VII. Socrates begins: The types of divine madness.

(243e-245c)

VIII. The immortality of the soul.

(245c-246a)

IX. Myth of the soul. The charioteer and two horses. The procession of souls.

(246a-247c)

X. The soul's vision of true Being. Its fall and incarnation.

(247c-248d)

XI. Reincarnation and final liberation of the soul. The philosopher's privilege.

(248d-249d)

XII. The soul's recollection of ideal Beauty.

(249d-250d)

XIII. Love as the re-growing of the soul's wings.

(250e-252c)

XIV. The various types of lover.

(252c-253c)

XV. The subjugation of lust. Love and counter-love.

(253c-256e)

XVI. The speech concluded with a prayer.

(256e-257b)"

(cf. Hackforth, 1972: v-vii).

These sub-divisions are self-explanatory, except, perhaps, "XI," what Hackforth calls "the philosopher's privilege." In sub-division "X" – where the "Law of Destiny" noted above is stated – Socrates had just finished enumerating the spectrum of re-incarnations for psychē, i.e. from highest incarnation as disposition toward philosophy to lowest as disposition to tyranny. What Hackforth calls "privilege" refers, then, to both *anamnēsis* and *palingenesis*; according to Socrates,

> For this reason it is just that only a philosopher's soul grows wings, since its *memory* [emphasis added] always keeps it as close as possible to those realities by

being close to which the gods are divine. A man who uses reminders [viz. *anamnēsis*] of these things correctly is always at the highest, most perfect level of initiation, and he is the only one who is perfect as perfect can be. He stands outside human concerns and draws close to the divine; ordinary people think he is disturbed and rebuke him for this, unaware that he is possessed by God. Now this takes me to the whole point of my discussion of the fourth kind of madness...
(1997h: 249c-d).

We will follow Marsilio Ficino's approach to the topics and themes of the *Phaedrus* most relevant for our purposes.

As Ficino noted "before Socrates can affirm that love restores us to heaven, he has to examine a number of things concerning the condition of the soul, both divine and human." (Ficino, 1981: 84-86). Thus, this section of the meditation will focus on part "VII" from Hackforth's *Phaedrus* sub-divisions. Though a commentary and discussion of the *Phaedrus* in its totality is, of course, beyond the scope of this meditation, the *scala à la divine mania*, so to speak, at minimum requires us to discuss the emanation of divine love, which awakens psychē to its *palingenesis*.

Divine Mania. There are four (4) different kinds of divine madness discussed in the *Phaedrus*. According to Socrates,

The prophetess of Delphi and the priestesses at Dodona are out of their minds when they perform that fine work of theirs for all of Greece ... The people who designed our language in the old days never thought of madness as something to be ashamed of or worthy of blame; otherwise they would not have used the word "manic" for the finest experts of all – the ones who tell the future – thereby weaving insanity into prophecy. They thought it was wonderful when it came as a gift of the god, and that's why they gave its name to prophecy; but nowadays people don't know the fine points, so they stick in a "t" and call it "mantic." (Plato, 1997h: 244b1-244c5).

Generation oriented madness, as noted above, does not receive the epitaph "holy." However, madness in "descent" differs from generation oriented madness. The madness which Orpheus embodies must descend, must test itself to awaken to itself; refusing to release the grip on love, through the maddening descent all else falls away, and ascending the madness is revealed as divine gift of love. Thus, celestial oriented madness deserves its characteristic descriptors "sacred," "divine," and "holy" (cf. Plato, 1997i: 18b4-d1).

Further, in comparing inspiration and enthusiasm with technique, Plato prefers the former. For example, "in both name and achievement, madness (mania) from a god is finer than self-control of human origin, according to the testimony of the ancient language givers." (Plato, 1997h: 244d2-4). Hence, Socrates continues to enumerate and explicate the divine manias.

> Next, madness can provide relief from the greatest plagues of trouble that beset certain families because of their guilt for ancient crimes: it turns up among those who need a way out; it gives prophecies and takes refuge in prayers to the gods and in worship, discovering mystic rites and purifications that bring the man it touches through to safety for this and all time to come. So it is that the right sort of madness finds relief from present hardships for a man it has possessed. (244d5-e5).

Whereas the first mania is "*telestic*," this mania is "prophetic." Further, the first type of mania is associated with Dionysus and the second with Apollo. In fact, there is a "close connection between the Apollonian shrine at Delphi and the philosophical self-knowledge required by Plato's Socrates." From this it has even been suggested that the "Apollonian prophecy is inseparable from philosophizing and, hence, from rhetoric in its expanded general sense..." (Uždavinys, 2011: 3).

Chapter V: The Mystery of the *Scala Amoris*

The next mania relates directly to the *Phaedrus* both in terms of Socrates providing an inspired speech and the very beauty of Plato's dialog itself. We hear,

> Third comes the kind of madness that is possession by the Muses, which takes a tender virgin soul and awakens it to a Bacchic frenzy of songs and poetry that glorifies the achievements of the past and teachs them to future generations. If anyone comes to the gates of poetry and expects to become an adequate poet by acquiring expert knowledge of the subject without the Muses' madness, he will fail, and his self-controlled verses will be eclipsed by the poetry of men who have been driven out of their minds. (245a1-b1; cf. Plato, 1997d: 534a1-c4).

We have seen this final phrase multiple times now in the discussion of the manias, i.e. the idea that a divine power pushes us "out of our minds." In the context of this meditation, it should be clear that insofar as the mind is directed instrumentally and technically toward generation, then divine mania soteriologically awakens us. It is as if, even if we try to refuse the call, the question itself reveals it. What are you trying to refuse? In other words, perhaps the others just can't hear it. Moreover, in your relation to it, you are already relating to it – that invisible nothing from the perspective of the others. You cannot undo selection from above, nor should we want to.

Of the four divine manias we are told that the fourth is different from the others. The fourth kind is "amatory" or "erotic" mania.

> Therefore the Platonic *philosopher*, *as* the *madman* [emphases added] who nurtures wings, is the dialectically transformed 'speaker' (the fallen soul en-charmed by the magic of *logos*) whose apparently mad desires and *erōtikē mania* are not so much directly sent from the gods as sparkling from within as a desire for the divine banquet and for wisdom. [However,] the

three other kinds of madness discussed in Plato's
Phaedrus ... [i.e.] poetic, *telestic*, and prophetic indeed
are sent by the gods. (Uždavinys, 2011: 2; cf. Jung
1977b: 450).

In other words, the difference regarding the fourth of the divine
manias is that it functions like a silent call. Its presence may be
directed either downward toward generation or upward toward
contemplation, and within such a context each chooses psychē's
trajectory.

Hence, to sum, the four manias are telestic, prophetic, poetic,
and amatory. They are associated respectively with Dionysus, Apollo,
the Muses, and Aphrodite or Eros, and "there is an abundant union,
conspiration, and alliance with each other of the gods who preside
over these manias." (Taylor, 1896: lii; cf. Rouget, 1985: 208). Despite
the way in which the fourth divine mania is different, all of them are
understood in terms of divine love. Thus we hear in the Neoplatonic
vocabulary of Plotinus these are "the four species of divine love [also
understood as] four Plotinian hypostases ... between the One and
Body – namely Intelligence, Reason, Opinion, and Nature." (Allen,
1984: 209). Moreover, as Taylor remarks quoting Hermias on this
aspect of the *Phaedrus*, all four of the manias apply to Orpheus.

In regard to the background of some of the terminology, the
following is helpful:

The *telestic* madness is anagogic, and leads the soul to
its forgotten origins through the theurgic rites of
ascent or other sacramental means of purification. The
inspired telestic liturgies (*telestikē, hieratikē
telesiourgia, theōphoria*) are not necessarily to be
regarded straightforwardly as "operations on the
gods," thus deliberately and incorrectly equating the
animated cultic statues located in the context of
particular ritual communications with the invisible
metaphysical principles themselves. (Uždavinys, 2011:
3; cf. Cheak, 2013).

"Anagoge" refers to the "interpretation of a word, passage, or text (as of Scripture or poetry) that finds beyond the literal, allegorical, moral senses a fourth and ultimate spiritual or mystical sense." (Merriam-Webster, 2015). Further, a few remarks are in order about the term "theurgy." In terms of its definition, it refers to "the art of technique of compelling or persuading a god or beneficent or supernatural power to do or refrain from doing something." (Merriam-Webster, 2015).

Just as "longing for [contemplation of eternal "Platonic" Ideas] is imagined as a yearning for wings and the regained ability to fly to the divine banquet. ... this pressing desire for wholeness, for noetic integrity, and for one's true divine identity..." (Uždavinys, 2011: 2), *what we do with the divine manias determines our relation to the divine* (cf. Pieper, 1995). In this context consider Nietzsche's concern for the *The Birth of Tragedy*. Recall, Nietzsche speaks of "the blissful ecstasy that wells from the innermost depths of man, indeed of nature, [and] at this collapse of the *principium individuationis*, we steal a glimpse into the nature of the *Dionysian*," and further, Nietzsche suggests such a glimpse may be "brought home to us most intimately by the analogy of intoxication" (Nietzsche, 1967:36). That is,

> In song and in dance man expresses himself as a member of a higher community; he has forgotten how to walk and speak and is on the way toward flying into the air, dancing. His very gestures express enchantment. ... *He is no longer an artist, he has become a work of art* [emphasis added]: in these paroxysms of intoxication the artistic power of all nature reveals itself to the highest gratification of the primordial unity. The noblest clay, the most costly marble, man, is here kneaded and cut, and to the sound of the chisel strokes of the Dionysian world-artist rings out the cry of the Eleusinian mysteries ... 'Do you sense your Maker, world?' (Nietzsche, 1967:37-38).

By pointing deeper into the "night wisdom" of the artist, a wisdom in which twilight and death are not forgotten, the communion in a "higher community" is entered, as if the *principium individuationis* had collapsed into the primordial center of lived experience. This "lived center," then, would be *henosis*.

Recall "enthusiasm," from above, i.e. ἐνθουσιασμός, speaks of be-ing filled with the divine substance of the gods. The difference, then, between the terms "demon" and "daimon" (sometimes spelled daemon) is that the material clinging orientation, as if determining a downward *disposition*ed, daimon is referred to as a "demon," and the daimon turned toward ascending retains the original term properly, i.e. "daimon." Turn-ing away from contemplating to generating shifts the daimonic to the demonic, e.g. Taylor clarifies with the locution "material demons" (Taylor, 1891: 56). And, recalling the Myth of Er, Hillman famously noted "The daimon ... does not go away." (Hillman, 1996: 8).

Mary P. Nichols rightly notes regarding Nietzsche's understanding of the world, "the world itself is the poetry of a god in pain, made bearable by his creation of a world of appearance that distracts him from his pain." (Nichols, 2010: 15). As I discussed in my first monograph *Full Throttle Heart: Nietzsche Beyond Either/Or*, put into the vocabulary of these meditations, from the point of ascension. i.e. the celestial point of view, the tragic is comic. In other words, the loss of Eurydice – though indeed tragic – Nietzsche would emphasize, ultimately conditions the revelation of the Orphic Theogony, the Mysteries, transformation into a divine "Shamanic" identity, and revelation of the path of liberation for his followers.

We should keep in mind the Orphic genealogy offered to us by Ficino at the beginning of this meditation as we read the following from Nichols: "Zarathustra explains that he used to suppose that the world was created by a suffering god who wanted to look away from its suffering. Now Zarathustra recognizes that it is humanity itself that creates gods in order to look away from its suffering." (Nichols, 2010: 15). What I would correct about this statement is that it is the "created" (i.e. created by/revealed by the Song of Orpheus?) that expresses the beauty and joy of existence for humans. Thinking of the *amor fati* theme in *The Cheerful Science*, it would be as if through the Song of Orpheus we too can be ones who "make things beautiful" (cf. Nietzsche, 1974: §276).

Finally, consider the following two ideas from Proclus' *Elements of Theology*: First, "While the gods are present alike to all things, not all things are present alike to them; each order is present in the degree of its capacity and enjoys them in the degree of its presence, which is the measure of its participation" (Proclus, 1816: 395; Sweeney,1982: 142). Second,

> A participant which is suitably disposed is not balked of its participation; so soon as a thing is ready for communion with them, straightaway they are present – not that in this moment they approached or till then were absent, for they are eternally unvarying. If, then, any terrestrial thing be fit to participate them, they are present even to it... (Proclus, 1816: 395; Sweeney, 1982: 142; cf. John 10:27).

In the context of our meditation on divine mania we may hear the above in terms of *palingenesis*. In other words, the activation/awakening of psychē's capacities may be understood as relating to the progress of its trajectory of liberation from the Wheel of (re)incarnation. The divine manias then are located at the point of contact with the divine insofar as we mortals can sustain the contact.

Ficino's articulation of the Platonic argument at work here is brilliant:

> To the extent that the soul turns toward itself and toward divine things and shows that it has its own motions, which may surmount the corporeal condition, it testifies too that it does not depend on the body and that it agrees with divine things and that therefore, separated from the body, it can live united with divinity. (Ficino, 1981: 88).

The idea of a "testament" with the divine as itself an indicator of one's contact with the divine speaks of the gifts of the first three manias and the ability to testify to the presence of the divine by mounting Eros and ascending the *scala amoris* toward the *mysterium coniunctionis* and *henosis* (cf. John 3 : 29-30).

This idea from Orpheus is not only clarified in Plato, others suggest it may be found in many religions and spiritual practices, including, for example, Christianity and Buddhism. According to a Reverend Henderson, from his book titled, *The Wheel of Life: A Study of Palingenesis in Its Relation to Christian Truth.*

> It is not only in Buddhism and the Indian religions, but in Christianity too [cf. (Matthew 19 :28)], that the ideal of selflessness [i.e. non-ego-complex driven love] is preached with all fervor. In the last the symbol of death has been used for expressing the idea of man's deliverance from the life that is not true. This is the same as Nirvana, the symbol of extinction of the lamp. (Tagore, 1915: 71-72; quoted in Henderson, 1931: 59).

Henderson goes on to clarify, "Nirvana is not necessarily the extinction of being; it is rather 'the extinction of that sinful, grasping, condition of mind and heart which would otherwise, according to the great mystery of Karma, be the cause of renewed mundane existence." (Henderson, 1931: 59-60). Thus, he concluded,

> Call it Nirvana; call it Heaven, or Paradise, the thought is still the same – deliverance from the imperfections of our frail humanity; the passing of those earth-born clouds which obscure the Face of the Eternal Sun of our Souls – the realization of ... the fountain of Life ... the Beatific Vision.(Henderson, 1931: 63).

Given the interesting parallels with the Cave Allegory and prompted here by Henderson, some general notes regarding Buddhism seem appropriate.

In a Buddhist vocabulary, the trajectory of this soteriology may be thought through by thinking: Samsara *to* the Four Noble

Truths *to* the Three Jewels of Buddhism (which include meditative practices leading to the experience of a "phenomenological reduction") *to* a contemplative life (*samahdi*) for the sake of further unfettering *to* nirvana "with spatiality" *to* only a small number of rebirths with nirvana while perfecting wisdom (*prajna*) as an *arhat* and enduring until *samyak sambuddha*, i.e. "final" nirvana.

Further, it is interesting to note that, according to the "Mindfulness of Breathing Sutra" from the *Middle Length Discourses* (118.15), the development and cultivation of "mindfulness of breathing" is supposed to be sufficient to achieve an awareness of nirvana. Within the context of this discussion such an awareness may be understood in terms of the *telestic*. The first stage toward nirvana is known as a "stream-entrant." (Hirakawa, 1990: 57). This is especially interesting regarding Heidegger's discussion of *Zug*, Plato's discussion of the "train" or "trail" (like a comet's tail) of the gods, and the idea of the term "mania" as "God approaching."

> "Leave me alone, unless you understand these things.
> The divine madness has expelled all human thoughts
> from my breast... now I can see the holy place swaying..."
> (*de raptu Proserpinae*, I. 4-8, Isbell,
> (Translation [slightly modified]).

> "Night light
> wakes me from a dream
> that seemed so long."
> ~Yayu (Trans. mod.)
> (*Japanese Death Poems*: 339).

Translation Notes to Orpheus, Eurydice, Hermes

Translation Notes to
Orpheus, Eurydice, Hermes

Translation notes placed at the end so as to not disrupt reading. Line numbers coincide with the German.

Line #4[1]
Line #20 "folds"[2]
Line #21[3]
Line #34[4]
Line #39[5]

---

[1] The German "Porphyr" refers to "fiery igneous," i.e. lava rock. Its dark (reddish) purple color is symbolically associated with royalty, death and mourning. It is at times also associated with the "super-natural," "spirituality" and "spirit" in that purple is the color of the spirit chakra and the top of the color spectrum.

[2] Double entendre of the folds of the cloak and of the strip of cotton.

[3] "Stringed instrument" here refers, of course, to the "lyre." There are two reasons I prefer "stringed instrument." One, many contemporary readers do not know to what the term "lyre" refers. Second, when hearing the poem read aloud in English audience members can easily mishear it, especially given the first reason. Though, it should be noted, as a number of philologists have pointed out, the term "lyre" may also refer to a book, i.e. titled "Lyre," which was rumored to have been written by Orpheus, (cf. de Jáuregui, et al., 2011: 148).

[4] The German here is difficult to render. The idea is something like, "they left too." Imagine you are to meet two people at some destination, and all of you are leaving from the same place. You're not allowed to look back to see if they are following you. You might say in a reassuring way to yourself – wondering if they left yet or at all – "No, I'm sure they left too." For conciseness, I deferred to Mitchell's rendering of "they had to be behind him." As I believe it appropriately portrays the concern of Rilke's Orpheus at the moment in question.

[5] Here is the often noted term "*das Zurückschaun*" the Backward Glance, the Turning Gaze of Orpheus, etc.

Line #40[6]
Line #44[7]
Line #53[8]
Line #60 "within herself"[9]
Line #60 "secret anticipation"[10]
Line #64 "beyond fulfillment"[11]
Line #69 "untouchable"[12]
Line #69 "flower"[13]
Line #74 "familiarity"[14]

---

[6] The polyphonic beauty of Rilke's German here simply cannot be translated into English. Consider Rilke's phrase *"müsste er sie sehen."* Notice the English "must" is a cognate here with *"müsste."* Hence, though the English translation correctly expresses the "surely he would see them" by capturing the necessity inherent in the "must," what the English misses is the sense in which the same language urgently expresses: "he must see them." This helps Rilke build anticipation toward the moment at line #85 which refers to the Backward Glance.

[7] This could also be translated as "wand" or "thyrsus," though staff seems less jarring to the context.

[8] Cf. "turned."

[9] Cf. "inward-looking," "self-consumed."

[10] Literally "as a higher hope," and perhaps "as one whose time has come" or "a woman near birth."

[11] Compare "gushing with death." Ultimately deferring here to Mitchell's rendering, though implications of flowing out or overflowing should be included.

[12] Respecting the distinctness of Rilke's lines, here; otherwise, "She was untouchable, in her new virginity."

[13] Initially I used "flower-bud"; however, "young" is more pregnant with connotation. Also, "closed" seems to do the work of "bud."

[14] This could be "intimacy" or "indiscretion," though the connotation of Hermes and knowledge seemed to resonate with "familiarity."

Comments Regarding *The Sonnets to Orpheus*

Comments Regarding *The Sonnets to Orpheus*

I had originally intended to make explicit translation notes – just like the ones above regarding Rilke's 1907 poem – on *The Sonnets to Orpheus*. However, I ultimately decided against it given its length. Rather, I've put together the following comments, in general, especially regarding Rilke's *Sonnets to Orpheus*.

§1 *Rilke's Polysemy: How to Read the Lines of the Sonnets*

There are so many examples throughout the *Sonnets* where Rilke's polysemy appears. At one point I considered titling this section "Rilke's Use of Quadruple Entendre." However, I would rather that we simply consider a few of the examples I have in mind so that readers might be able to view the poems as I viewed them into translation.

I will say, though, in regard to the idea of quadruple entendre. The *Sonnets* may be read as speaking to different entities. The four (4) entities I recognize are: Orpheus, Eurydice, the Reader of the Sonnets, and the developing aspects of the phantasmagoria of Orpheus' song. This last entity is variously characterized as: the earth, nature in general, various aspects of nature (such as trees and flowers), or the changing of the seasons.

Thus, Rilke's poetry may be seen in its polysemic grandeur when the entity to whom the lines are spoken becomes ambiguous. On the one hand, there are times when it seems multiple entities may be intended simultaneously. On the other hand, there are times when – along the lines of the experience of a haiku poem – silence is needed to allow the polysemy to more clearly manifest.

I came to the Rilke poems steeped in haiku poetry, and had – in 21015 – given multiple lectures on the dynamics of haiku poetry, even presenting at a conference on the relationship between the philosophy of Martin Heidegger and the specific haiku known as Japanese death poetry. Thus, I immediately noticed that depending on how I chose to cut the lines of Rilke's poems influenced the meaning that his poetry rendered possible.

The rule I followed for this was to stay as close as possible (as if taking up a literal translation in regard to the line structure) to Rilke's actual German line breaks. However, I would also consider each sonnet as if it were a message. This often meant translating each sonnet twice – once as if it were a poem and once as if it were a philosophical paragraph. I would, then, construct the poem – *cutting the lines as needed* – in order to capture what I continue to call the polysemic grandeur of the *Sonnets.*

Here are some examples. Recall that when reading haiku, the idea is to pause after reading each line. The first example I chose is *the first stanza of the third sonnet.* Notice what my choice regarding where to cut the lines accomplished. On the one hand, by cutting the line at the word "how," the first line reads as if it were both a question and a statement. On the other hand, the cutting of the second line amplifies both of the potential readings of the first line.

> A god can do it. But tell me, how
> should a man follow after him
> through the narrow lyre?

Thus, multiple meanings emerge simultaneously. In other words, "How can a god do it?" "Should a man follow after him?" "How should a man follow after him?" And, then these same last two questions echo for "through the narrow lyre?" This pattern can be seen animating the second stanza too.

Next, consider *Sonnet §10*. Rilke poetically points to a distinction between a force of animation and the figure through which that force moves. "Do we know, friends, or do we not? That which shapes this lesson in hesitation as the features of a human face." This "lesson in hesitation," at least, doubly refers to the hesitation "moving" within the initial line of the last stanza, as it makes meaning, and the hesitation also refers to the hesitation of those initiated to enter the lament world. Further, the distinction seems to connect with the famous motif from *Sonnet §11* by suggesting that we are that which "rides" the force of animation as it moves through the figure of the Orpheus & Eurydice Myth – like a voice singing a song. Lastly, two comments regarding where the lines are cut.

First, by cutting the third line at "heart," each of the lines that follow it may be read as referring back to it. And, with the same pattern moving up that stanza, the "rose and flowed," then, takes on four different references and, thereby, meanings. (1) The eulogy of Orpheus rose and flowed; (2) the silver ore rose and flowed; (3) the heart of Orpheus rose and flowed; (4) the never-ending wine of Orpheus rose and flowed.

> Eulogy, that's it! Called to eulogize,
> he rose and flowed
> like silent silver ore from stone. His heart,
> ah, a fleeting wine press of never-ending wine,
> for us alone.

Next, consider *the first stanza of the twenty-fifth sonnet*. Notice, again, how the cutting of the lines contributes to allowing the polysemy to rise and flow.

> You, whom I knew like a flower whose name
> I didn't know, you were about to evaporate.
> I will remember you, now, one last time,
> and describe you to them, beautiful playmate
> of the insurmountable scream.

Here, the "I didn't know" functions in both lines one and two. That is, "I knew you like a flower whose name I didn't know," and "I didn't know you were about to evaporate." If we knew the name of the flower, would we have known she was going to evaporate? And, had we known she was going to evaporate, would it have changed anything for us?

This movement is mirrored at the terminological level, rather than the structural level of the stanza, in the remaining lines. Notice the contrast between "beautiful playmate" and "insurmountable scream." Just like "I knew" and "I didn't know," the lightheartedness of "playmate" contrasts with the idea of an inevitable and "insurmountable scream" (cf. Sonnet §34). Moreover, in regard to the larger, overall, narrative of the sonnets, these contrasts contribute to the idea of a deep ambiguity regarding the meaning of the Myth of Orpheus.

Lastly, in regard to "I will remember you, now, one last time, and describe you to them" consider the following. Not only does the "you" function beautifully – and playfully – as an ambiguous placeholder term, there is a sense in which it, of course, refers to Eurydice. Now, to whom will she be described? To us, of course, and, yet, to whom does "us" refer?

Lastly, consider the final two stanzas of *the forty-ninth sonnet*, that is, *Sonnet 23* of the *2nd Series*.

> Afraid, we reach out only for a hold,
> sometimes, we're too young for what is old,
> and too old for that which never was.

> We are only where we praise nonetheless.
> Because, oh, we are the knot and the blade,
> and the sweetness of a ripening hazard.

In regard to the first of these two stanzas, notice that cutting the lines, as I did, gives "sometimes" a pivotal double entendre status. "Sometimes we reach out for a hold," and "sometimes we're too young..." Further, in regard to the overall ambiguity of the Myth of Orpheus that emerges toward the end of the sonnets, "too young for what is old" and "too old for that which never was" both, contrastingly, point to the phantasmagoria of Eurydice. They also turn back, so to speak, and refer to the fear that initiates this stanza. The remaining section of this chapter and the final section of the postface will speak to the insight of the overall ambiguity of the Myth of Orpheus.

In the final stanza, to say that "we are only where we praise," points to the eulogizing of Orpheus, and the word "nonetheless" recalls the contrast between being too young and too old and, thereby, the fear. The last two lines of this stanza, then, invoke the notion of the Gordian Knot, and – again by way of contrasting references – suggest that we are the Gordian Knot of the fear and the phantasmagoria; and, the progression through its mythical structure – its "ripening" – is both a sweetness and a hazard.

§2 *A Mystery of Eurydice: She is (Always) Already Dead*

There are two insights that came to me by way of translating these poems. The first is that Eurydice is always already dead as the Myth of Orpheus & Eurydice begins. The second is that the "overall" meaning of the Myth may, ultimately, be ambiguous. On the one hand, I believe both of these insights contribute significantly to a deeper understanding of the Myth. On the other hand, the second insight, specifically, contributes significantly toward seeing the absolute profundity of the Myth.

In regard to the first insight, the Myth of Orpheus & Eurydice opens with the death of Eurydice. In terms of the Mysteries of Eurydice, there are two mysteries to consider here. First, this insight resonates with the Eleusinian and other Sacred Mysteries of the ancient Greeks in that it invokes the idea that embodiment is a kind of death for the soul. When the revelations begin, we are already dead. Second, love understood in terms of physicality initiates the movement of Orpheus, and, therefore, the en-trance into the fugue of Orpheus manifests in relation to the death of Eurydice.

This insight has, in my opinion, profound consequences for understanding the Myth of Orpheus, especially the Moment when Orpheus "looks back" at Eurydice. To state it directly: the loving interactions that take place with Eurydice in the Myth of Orpheus & Eurydice all take place within the phantasmagoria of Orpheus' lament song. As Novalis told us, "Death is the romanticizing principle." And, as Kierkegaard pointed out to us, to see the beloved from the point of view of death is a kind of repetition (that is, of the figure of Orpheus). We must see her as gone for her to return to us in her highest form of loving.

Yet, when she returns to us in the highest form of loving of which she is capable – I am not speaking of motherly terrestrial love, I am speaking of disembodied celestial love – she returns to us *as dead*. Thus, the profundity of the Myth of Orpheus & Eurydice can be envisioned through the mystery that Eurydice is always already dead. For, if she is not, then the Myth does not begin; if she is not, then it is not the lament song of Orpheus.

The second insight with which we began this section of the chapter is the idea that the overall meaning of the Myth may be, ultimately, ambiguous. We can see this by juxtaposing the comments regarding the Mystery of Eurydice. One of the questions that always torments readers of the Myth of Orpheus & Eurydice is: Why does Orpheus look back at Eurydice?

According to the reading I am revealing here, *Orpheus looks back at Eurydice because he remembers that she is dead.* The Eurydice that Orpheus is guiding out of the Underworld is a construction of his lament song. This shade of Eurydice belongs to the phantasmagoria which manifest through his grief. It is the manifestation of his mourning. On the one hand, it is not the real Eurydice. On the other hand, because Eurydice is always already dead, she is truly gone. There is no retrieving her from the Deathlands.

This speaks directly to the ambiguity of the Myth as a whole, then, in that the Myth – it seems to me now – should be understood more as the movement through a fugue, the movement through a dreamlike phantasmagoria of lament. This is not so much the experience of reality as it is the process of the loss of Eurydice. In other words, the truth of each phase of the process is just as real as the truth of every other phase. To pass through the fugue is to live the truth of each phase.

I take this to be profound, then, especially because when we live through the phase in which we feel the joy and hope of the experience of rescuing Eurydice, those feelings are real. Now, from some abstract "external" point of view – for example, of someone not moving through the fugue, that is, someone who cannot hear the music, the lament song of Orpheus – it could be said that the entire experience is an illusion. Orpheus is "imagining" the experience of Eurydice and commemorating her into a displaced shade figure by eulogizing her in a lament song.

However, from the point of view of someone moving through the lament song, from the point of view of someone moving through the fugue, from the point of view of someone moving through the figure (archetype) of the Myth of Orpheus & Eurydice, the abstract external point of view is eclipsed; each phase of the fugue's movement is *felt and experienced*, and, therefore, the truth of the lived experience is that of each phase of the Myth. In this way, we would say that the "overall" meaning of the Myth is, ultimately, ambiguous, because it is not simply possible to *look back* at the end of the Myth and claim it has merely one meaning. Rather, *looking back* at the end of the Myth is one more phase in relation to the Myth.

> He said to himself, they had to be behind him;
> *said it aloud and heard it die away.*
> They had to be behind him,
> but their steps were torturously soft...
> If only he could turn around, just once,
> (but would looking back not decompose
> this entire work, so near completion) ...
> ~Rilke, "Orpheus, Eurydice, Hermes"

From what we are calling the "external" point of view, that is, the point of view of someone who, while not moving through the figure of Orpheus, is witnessing someone else move through it, it may be said that "it has to end eventually." For, everything (in the physical dimension) has an expiration date. However, the experience from within the lament song of Orpheus is different. For example, even having that same insight regarding expiration could function, from within the experience, to fuel the "romanticizing" of Eurydice.

Thus, to initiate the Myth, Eurydice is always already dead, and her death is both the motor force for the lament song and the very truth of the song which allows us to look back and recognize Eurydice within it as a shade.

§3 *Looking Back: Killing Our Love, I Watched You Become merely an Idea*

Panic allows you to see love in a different light, but seeing love in that light may change the way you relate to it. The mystery can be stated as a kind of paradox. On the one hand, it is only through losing you that I am able to see you again. On the other hand, it is my seeing you again that causes me to lose you.

Perhaps it is true that to attach to you is to attach to an idea of you, and, then, as the spell of the attachment breaks and the object of desire evaporates, I am able to witness that "you" – the you to which I was attached – was *always already* merely an idea. And, yet, because I am unaware of this truth during *the time of the attachment*, the evaporation is experienced genuinely through grief. It is a process of mourning that is no less real for being phantastic.

This is yet another – different – answer to the question: Why does Orpheus "look back" at Eurydice? To state the answer succinctly in terms of the mortals who hang in the balance of Persephone's offer to Orpheus, embodiment can only sustain the reflection of the Orpheus constellation for a time. That is, it can only sustain it during *the time of attachment*.

Souls enter into the Spring, mud merging with mud and souls passing through the Houses of the Dead. As Summer ends, the mud bonds dry and break. Yet, something tells us – Orpheus tells us, that is, Orpheus hears something in his own song; Orpheus witnesses the power of his own charm – and this secret preserves us... We initiates... With the greatest of respect: Persephone is a witch. Her imprisonment in the eternal Daughter-Mother recurrence has imbibed her with the dark arts of the Deathlands. It *is* the sound of the wind in your cloak. It is a trick Orpheus. It is a trick that you willingly underwent.

And, as you wake in the midst of this phantasmagoria of mourning, you learn that: To break the spell, you must break your heart.

Yet, even the rocks, they hurled at you, turned tender with hearing... your song. For, though it is with your own song that Persephone bewitches you, when you break your heart, you realize what parts of it can't be broken. When you break your heart, you recognize the tenderness of the god looking back at you in the eternal Lover-Beloved recurrence.

Why does this god look back at us? Why won't this god simply let us re-incarnate? Is it that, somehow, we have been forgiven the sins of our past lives? Their karma has burned out? Or, have we passed the true test of love? We have learned to carry love into death. I will sacrifice myself for the truth of love. I will sacrifice myself because I know the truth of love.

§4 *Grief Belongs to the Body: I Remembered You as long as I Could, and, Now, I Can't Remember You...*

     If I am this spirit... This spirit haunting this body...
Then, I came into this body, just to remember you... one more time....
The body allows me to manifest a phantasmagoria... it allows me to project a world... a lament world... an unreal world...
a world in which I can see you... one more time...
And, yet, it is the eternal nature of these bodies to recycle...
To be, created, anew... with the memories of any past incarnation of this spirit *dying away* with every manifested body...
     This is the only way I can love you forever...
Just as I must take another breath to sing your presence into being, I cannot simply hold my breath... "For the truth of singing, is another breath... A breath of nothing... My mournful expiration..." I must re-turn to the experience of your death, so that I can experience your return to me... in this song... I must sing it... I must say it aloud...

              ...so says Orpheus...

             Said It Aloud
             And Heard It
             Die Away

Table of Contents

Postface

At the risk of it sounding like hyperbole: translating these poems has extracted a significant toll from me. There was a strange sense in which my experience of life was somehow attached to whichever was the last sonnet I had translated. This was especially menacing to me in that, for example, I would spend weeks translating one sonnet.

My method for the 1907 poem was to approach it in a frenzy. To approach it with my heart, while I was frantic. This is precisely how the name "Orpheus Moment" spontaneously manifested in my speech. The Orpheus Moment refers to that moment in a love relationship when you realize the other is gone. When your defenses – for whatever reason – can no longer distract you from your desire to reach out and touch them, from your desire to hear their voice, and to look into their eyes.

Of course, that moment belongs to Orpheus, as its purest and highest expression, because that moment is fully illuminated with the truth that our beloved is gone. We can no longer touch them; we can no longer use our ears to relate to the spontaneity of their voice; we can no longer use our eyes to track the spontaneity of the look in their eyes. In this way, the Orpheus Moment may also be thought of as the perfect coupling of love and death.

If the thoughts brought to mind by the poem did not bring my heart to ache with longing, to feel a kind of breathless panic regarding an empty future, then I considered my translation to be merely a draft. Tears and nausea were the signs that it was worthy of the emotional pain of Orpheus.

My method for translating the *Sonnets* of 1922 was oddly quite different. The time between the two projects – for Rilke – is supposed to indicate his shift away from sentimentality; scholars, of course, blame this "maturity," in part, on the influence of working with Rodin.

In this way, the 1922 sonnets are longer and more intricate (and therefore more complicated) than the 1907 poem. As I will address below, there are points in Rilke's *Sonnets* where he raises the polysemy (that is, the coexistence of many possible meanings for his words and phrases) to a feverish pitch. As I have already noted elsewhere, it reminds me of a fugue.

It was difficult to sustain Rilke's, for example, quadruple entendre in translation. Whereas the 1907 poem took me a month, the 1922 sonnets took me years. I will state here in one sentence what was three pages in my first draft: I feel as though the spirit of Orpheus somehow helped me translate these poems. I know how that sounds; trust me, I know how that sounds; and, yet, I truly feel that way; it truly felt that way. Hence, my method for translating the 1922 poems felt very much like using Rilke's Sonnets as hints to help me recognize the path Orpheus illuminates... out of the phantasmagoria... out of the haunted tomb...

§1 *Panic Illuminates a World*

Where did you go? What has happened to my love? To feel time constricting around you. To become short of breath. To witness focus scramble between the feeling of a sudden weight on your chest and the sudden awareness of an emptiness vast enough to annihilate your memories in an instant.

Who do you love? Of course, you remember, right? Machines cannot love you. If I am merely surrounded by machines, then from where does this belief in love come? Orpheus. To be closed within this call-and-response song, and, yet, the vast openness – fettered as we still are – shows us the way to a higher death.

These machines are dead, but they have never truly lived. We followed the sound of the lyre. We learned to hear, and the song we heard taught us a higher truth. Yes, you learned that you are a song. Who sings it? And, you learned to hear the emptiness in which that song resounds.

Now, when the song begins to play, we witness its affect. And, yet, we remember; that is to say, we do not repeatedly forget; we remember what happens when the song ends. We remember how the machines behave, and we remember how they forget us. What does their forgetting unveil for us?

These machines mindlessly chatter on... Are we all alone, despite being surrounded by each other? Must we be remembered, must we be recognized, to not be alone?

§2 *The View of Love in the Mirror of Death*

Forgetting is natural. The issue is not the forgetting, the issue is the tempo of the forgetting. What would you do – what could you do – if suddenly you realized that you no longer forget at the rate at which others forget? More to the point, how could you not see them as machines? What would you do with the experience of a loss that no one else seems to be able to experience? Why can't others experience it? Because they forget too much, before they can mourn.

I remember in my youth wanting to be more disciplined so that I could sit for long periods of time and produce art. Eventually I reached that level of dedication and sacrifice. After the thrill of feeling such surges of creativity, I just wanted to be "human" again. Yet, that too, now, is a myth, and we cannot go back. Besides, when were we ever human?

I see machines resonating with each other in their inauthenticity. Like two radios playing the same station, each recognizes something of itself in the other without recognizing itself. These people don't really love each other, I think to myself. And, yet, they "have" love. To "be" love. What is that? That is loss, or so it seems in this mirror of death. Perhaps I'm just jealous; jealous of them, because: they don't yet realize that they're dead.

I really want to believe all the things I say. I no longer know if I am upset because I cannot believe them, or if I am upset because they cannot be true. It is not that the others don't believe them. They believe them. Yet, for all that, it does not produce the result for which I hoped.

For them, it's simply time to forget... again. For me, the light is much brighter now. In this light, it is much easier to see the reflection as reflection and the mirror as a dying surface.

§3 *The Madness of Being Haunted by What is Gone*

Perhaps the first panic attack is the purest. During all the other panic attacks you have some awareness of what is happening in general terms, some objective awareness, and it somehow reduces the intensity of panic. No wonder we cling to objectivity; no wonder we cling to reason. Anything to reduce the panic of beginning to awaken inside this tomb.

Postface

Eurydice is dead. The spontaneity that was her, outside of us, is gone. And, now, only the spontaneity of panic propelling memories toward us remains. There is no doubt that this is an experience of being haunted. Who haunts us? It is Eurydice who haunts Orpheus. It is Eurydice who appears in the phantasmagoria of his lament song. And, yet, she is gone.

Eurydice is dead. We chase her until we realize we are chasing a phantom. *When we realize we are chasing a phantom we are left with the realization that we can no longer tell the difference between the appearance of this phantom and what we once took to be the real Eurydice.*

Of course, our experience of her was always conditioned by our senses and the limits of our capacity to understand. For, if we are colorblind, then we saw her in limited colors. Certainly, spontaneity is not the only aspect of the experience of her that made it real? For, even the most spontaneous people settle into a predictable spontaneity. What does that even mean? That in precise terms what we experience of these spontaneous people is their spontaneity, and, yet, we become habituated to their spontaneity. That's what it means to think of the spontaneity of a machine.

Ugh, Eurydice is dead. No philosophical definition, no precise terminology can resurrect, or even recreate, those smiles we shared, those laughs we shared. And, yet, I cannot help but recognize that these are memories – right now. Perhaps the closest we can come to that resurrection is the pain of mourning the loss. Ah, the wisdom of Orpheus. The lament song as an attempt to hold onto her, before the turning machine parts in this tomb erase even the memories of her.

Eurydice is dead. This pain is one last attempt to embrace... what? Who?

Wait. What about that colorblind comment? Even if there was a real Eurydice spontaneously causing the images of her to appear to me, I was relating to images of her. I was relating to whatever through me could appear, and I have no way to climb outside myself to see if these representations of her somehow match her exactly.

Well, there is a way to climb outside of myself, to climb outside of this tomb; however, in order to check if these representations match her exactly, I must turn back and look at her; I must look at her during our ascent. Ah, the Orpheus Moment. Why do I want the truth? Why do I want it to be real?

Yes, it is the desire for truth and reality that has ruined it all. It is the desire for truth and reality that has illuminated the ruins through which we ascend in this tomb. Orpheus, that is, will show us the truth of the path – it is the absolute nature of this constellation – if we listen more deeply to his song. And, all who can hear his song, eventually, listen more deeply. All who can hear his song, follow its lament into a depth where we scream.

§4 *Screaming Into the Abyss: Greeting the Forces That Disdain to Destroy You*

Here is one last poem that I have translated from Rilke. These are the rightly celebrated, famous, first lines of the first of the *Duino Elegies*:

> "Who, if I cried out, would hear me
> among the angelic hierarchy? and even if one should,
> suddenly take me to his heart: I would be extinguished
> by the intensity of his existence. For beauty is nothing
> but the beginning of terror we can only just endure,

and we adore it because it serenely disdains
to destroy us. Every angel is terrifying.
    And so, if I choke back the call of my dark sobs,
who is able to give me what I need? Not angels,
not people, and not the resourceful animals,
for they already notice that
we are not very reliably at home
                    in our interpreted world.

Our "interpreted world"? To what does that refer? It refers to how we make meaning of these images appearing in our tomb, appearing-through our embodiment. In regard to the Myth of Orpheus and Eurydice, it is the phantasmagoria produced by the lament song of Orpheus. We descend in it like Orpheus, seeking Eurydice, and we ascend in it as we climb the *scala amoris*.

It is the embrace of Orpheus, as he takes us to his heart. For, we know who would hear us, if we cried out. We know, now, because the very one who would hear is the one who gave us the ability to scream: Orpheus.

Orpheus' intensity is overwhelming. The presence of the beauty of our love relation is already the beginning of the terror that is the Orpheus Moment. And, so, as he pulls us toward his heart, the intensity increases to the point of panic, and, in the Orpheus Moment, we look back and scream...

Can anyone truly hear this scream? Perhaps we cannot even appreciate the depth of this scream, for it signals a profound annihilation. What is perhaps most difficult for us to appreciate regarding this annihilation that speaks through us is that with so much focus on Eurydice we do not recognize this moment as our own annihilation. For we are already extinguished in the *sparagmos* of Orpheus.

The intensity of Orpheus is the light that illuminates the path of the *scala amoris*; the intensity of Orpheus is the panic we feel in the Orpheus Moment; the intensity of Orpheus is his *sparagmos* in which we are transformed in death... This tomb, this pain, what of us remains?

§5 *The Paradoxical Secret of the Witch Who Actually Loved Me: In the Place of Greatest Abandonment, We Are Reminded of our Divinity*

I have re-worked and re-written this final section multiple times over the past almost two months now. Thus, of what follows, we might say it is a viewing in retrospect. It is a "looking back" at the work, so near completion. From this point of view, and to conclude, then, I will make three comments. Lastly, by "Myth" I do not mean "falsehood." I mean a polysemic narrative (*Mythos*) whose logic differs from that of the *Logos*.

The first comment, then, is in regard the Sacred Mysteries of the Ancient Greeks. The second is in regard to the experience of "fugue states." And, the third, on the one hand, speaks directly to the title of this section; on the other hand, it is the synthesis of the first two parts of this concluding section *and* the existential idea which I consider the culmination of my research into the Myth of Orpheus & Eurydice.

In regard to the Sacred Mysteries of the Greeks. As a point of departure, we should recall that the Eleusinian Mysteries are older than the Orphic Mysteries. This is easily confirmed by the position of Persephone in the Myth of Orpheus & Eurydice. That is to say, Persephone is (always) already in the Underworld – already the "Queen of the Dead" – before Orpheus makes his descent.

Further, recall that the Myth of Persephone and Demeter is also a story of yearning and loss and grief. In brief, it is as if, blind male desire abducts the daughter, Persephone, away from the mother, Demeter. Eventually Persephone escapes the Underworld, to be reunited with her mother, and the cycle of her leaving and returning to the Underworld – the initiates to the Sacred Mysteries seemed to believe – accounts for the changing of the seasons experienced by mortals.

The question, then, is how does the daughter escape Hades... the one who abducted her? We recall that Demeter roamed the land and even resorted to – as the Myth clearly states – a strategy of "scorched earth" to rescue her daughter. Yet, it was Persephone who broke the spell. For, Persephone – the Queen of the Dead – is also a breaker of lament spells. How did she accomplish her ascension out of the Underworld? She convinced Hades (the King of the Underworld) to impregnate her.

As the Myth goes, her offspring allows her to dwell outside the Underworld with her mother, Demeter, during Spring and Summer, before returning to the Underworld for Autumn and Winter. As I've emphasized in other publications, of all the characterizations of her offspring, it is especially interesting to Platonic philosophers to note that her offspring may be understood as Dionysus himself.

So, how is this relevant to the discussion of Orpheus? To state it directly: there is an art – passed down from mother to daughter, so to speak – of bewitching male energy. If we wanted to state it diabolically, we could say, this art is the motor force that keeps the Demeter-Persephone Cycle moving. It is both the art of a mother and the art of a daughter. It is the art of instilling love... its origin is from a female to a male.

Just like the polysemic nature of Rilke's poems expressing the polysemic nature of the Myth of Orpheus, the value of this witchcraft is not easily judged. Perhaps we might even say it is "undecidable." However, we can see that it is the original mechanism used to "escape the Underworld." And, from the point of view of Persephone, we might say that it is the same witchcraft that bewitched Orpheus. We will return to this line of thought after briefly discussing "fugue states."

ꢧ ꢧ ꢧ ꢧ ꢧꢧ ꢧ ꢧ ꢧ ꢧ

How strange it is to wake from a fugue state. How strange it is to realize you have thought you were relating to another person, and, then, you realize you were relating to a figment of your imagination. You have been relating to a projection.

Projection, here, means that you have projected an identity onto another person and have been relating to that identity, rather than to the actual other person. Though it is, perhaps, clinically incorrect to call this a "fugue state," I prefer that term for many reasons.

The most relevant of which, here, is that it is possible for us to construct an entire perception of reality grounded in the identity we project onto another person. Thus, we are attempting to function within a fabricated version of reality, since we are not operating with a reality-based perception of the other person.

When we come to realize this, it can be quite shocking at first, especially the initial realization that the person we are thinking about doesn't really exist. And, that person, in fact, never did exist.

Who should I thank for bringing me to this insight? Should I go find the body of that girl on whose surface I saw the mirage reflected? What would I say to her? It is not only a problem that she would, most likely, hear it as a move in a game; rather, to state it through the figure of Orpheus, she is dead.

Perhaps she could understand the logic of what I am saying. Perhaps she could understand the theory of what I am saying. However, she does not have the experiential knowledge of the Orphic-kind of loss. In fact, to accurately characterize this kind of loss the word I used previously ("mirage") may actually be an incorrect term.

And, this is another major reason why I like the term "fugue state." That is, just as nature's bloom is seasonally relative, so too the experiential reality of Eurydice is temporally relative. In other words, during the experience of attempting to retrieve her from the Underworld – from the Deathlands – we are relating to her: to this "shade" of a woman.

During that time, it is still not clear to us whether we will retrieve her from the Underworld or not. Thus, not only is our experience of her shady but real; it is also true that we relate to a future that includes her. *As if to say, "We cannot imagine a future without her in it."* Because, for us mortals, every future is naturally a projection, to envision a futural-Eurydice (envisioning Eurydice with us in the future) covers over her shadiness in the present.

The point at which we turn and see her as merely a shade is precisely the Orphic Turn. At that moment – just as in the Orpheus Myth – two revelations occur. The first is that Eurydice is dead, and we have only been with a shade. The second is the revelation of the *scala amoris* (cf. *2nd Series, Sonnet 13*).

Frank Scalambrino

In other words, think into and attempt to empathize with Orpheus at this moment. Most commentaries focus only on the first revelation, the grief and mourning. Yet, at the same time, in this moment of greatest abandonment, this moment when Orpheus recognizes he is alone in the Deathlands, he also realizes that he is a half-god; for, he used his powers to descend into the Hell of the Deathlands and has managed to transcend its curse of forgetfulness (cf. the River Lethē).

How strange it seems in the Orpheus Moment to realize that in breaking one's heart, to break the lament spell, one advances into the revelation of love's ineffability. This can be stated figuratively in terms of "the paradoxical secret of the witch who actually loved me."

The witch who actually loved me showed me the contrived, natural and, yet, practiced, depths of the Mother-Daughter Love Spell. She showed me that it is a spell and it is a trick. Its conjuration does not change the truth of the Deathlands. Those in the Deathlands remain dead. They are (always) already dead.

This witch – this amazing and beautiful witch with her pure heart – walked me through the stages of the Mother-Daughter Love Spell, while leaving out the ingredient of water from the River Lethē. Thus, as she concluded the ritual, I learned the secret usually reserved for mothers and daughters. And, though the secret proved the illusory nature of love on the lower end of the *scala amoris*, there was some tremendous sense in which it also proved the truth of the love on the higher end of the *scala amoris*. For, showing me the falsity of love, her pure heart was no longer eclipsed.

She showed me the divine silence in which the lament song of Orpheus takes place – the divine silence of ineffable love. To borrow a phrase from the *Secret Doctrine* 2:378, it is as if the pure heart of the witch allowed us "to approach the divine without being incinerated by its lower emanations." Of course, this itself invokes Orpheus as a magician and healer.

In "the magical tradition, three ideas about Orpheus are emphasized." It is worth quoting this passage at length.

> First, he is a psychopomp [a guide for souls to the place of the dead] and controls the afterlife of the soul because he is allied with or knows how to manipulate celestial or chthonic powers or both. Secondly, his lyre is the clue to his power. Its seven strings symbolize the seven planets, seven heavens, seven archons, and the divine cosmic harmony. It is not merely symbolic harmony, however, but is magically able to induce it; for a symbol, to the magically minded, is never a mere representation, but also a means of producing an effect. Thirdly, Orpheus is often called a healer, which is to say in a different way, a master of natural forces and producer of effects. (Vicari, 1982:73).

Thus, in the "magical tradition," or style of interpreting "the personages of classical fable are astral divinities who rule the universe. That means that they are ultimate natural principles that might be spoken of as angels, demons (or daimons), or 'archons' (rulers of the celestial spheres)." (Vicari, 1982:72). Hence, we find, according to "the oldest myth regarding Orpheus" that he "was a mighty magician," his sound was "associated with the moon," and he could sing dragons to sleep (Vicari, 1982:73).

In what way, then, is it the case that "In the place of greatest abandonment, we are reminded of our divinity"? The witch and I discussed the following Buddhist parable; it comes from §42 of Rinpoche's *Progressive Stages of Meditation on Emptiness*:

> There is a story about a man who went to a magician's [a witch's] home and was offered a cup of tea, and he took a sip of it. What he did not know was that the magician had put a spell in the tea, so no sooner had he put his cup down than he was under the sway of a magical illusion. He took to his horse and rode to the end of the world where there was a great ocean, and so he could go no further. He met a beautiful woman whom he married and by whom he had three children. He lived with her happily for three years until, falling upon bad times, he was driven to despair and threw himself into the ocean. At that point, the effect of the spell wore off, and he found himself back at the magicians' house with his tea still in front of him. So little time had passed, that the tea had not stopped swirling in the cup after he had put it down.

Though I was the one who provided this parable for us to discuss, interestingly, it was the witch's daughter who sent me the Secret Doctrine excerpt, noted above.

Now, in our discussion, the witch expressed her disagreement with the parable. At the same time, I felt quite strongly in agreement that the motivation associated with the Orpheus Cycle, so to speak, and the panic that once motivated the construction of this book were affects of an illusion – a magical spell cast by someone of questionable benevolence.

It was in the experience of falling in love, then, that the witch called forth the ancient wisdom of the Sacred Mysteries. What was missing from our conversations of the parable was – ironically, since I was writing this book at the time – the *scala amoris*. For example, as a kind of hermeneutic, the *scala amoris* allows us to recognize the lower levels of love, subjectively interpreted, as physical – to function in the natural "way of it" – as a kind of spell passed on from mother to daughter for the sake of preserving their cycle. At the same time, it allows us an awareness of the higher levels of love to which we may gain access through our recognition of the lower levels as the conjuration of illusions (cf. Sonnets 6 & 7, eulogize ≈ romanticize).

In this context, let us briefly recall Sonnet #25. The panic is a gate. The heart is a gate. And, perhaps initiation requires a form of heartbreak. We must pass through the terror, if we are to pass through the gate:

> You, whom I knew like a flower whose name
> I didn't know, you were about to evaporate.
> I will remember you, now, one last time,
> and describe you to them, beautiful playmate
> of the insurmountable scream.
> ~Rilke (Scalambrino translation) *1ˢᵗ Series, Sonnet 25*

The heartache of the traveler takes place before the illusion evaporates. Remembering her one last time, he can recognize the spiritual powers at work in her revelation as the beauty with him playing in the abyss... playing to the point of screaming a scream more spiritually necessary than can be perceived from within the illusion. It needs to be a scream so painful that it pushes you out of the illusion. A fated – fatal – scream...

To answer the question, then: It is of our very nature and essence to never be abandoned by God. In other words, the gods do not abandon us. As mortals we are created to be in their service, and we are bound to them. It is we who lose sight of them, though they are eternally (t)here.

Just as Orpheus is located at the top of the *scala amoris*, looking downward into the Deathlands, after the Orphic Moment in the Myth of Orpheus & Eurydice, so too our heartbreak pushes us out of the illusion at the lower end of the *scala amoris*. Yet, when this initiation rite is traversed correctly, we are not cast out of love. Rather, the initiation itself is initiation into the higher expressions of love... into the Sacred Mystery of Love.

At the end of the Orphic Moment in the Myth of Orpheus & Eurydice Orpheus stands atop the *scala amoris* in the excruciating glory of his abandonment. Whether intentional or not, Orpheus is abandoned by Eurydice. He is left alone to figure out the loss. Looking back over the Orpheus Cycle, the Spring-ing and the Fall-ing of the lament world... He is the invitation to initiation into the Mystery of Love, while eternally enduring fallen love.

It is the same for the initiates. When we look back... a(-)cross our initiation, traversing these stages through which we were liberated from fallen love into the Mystery of Love, we recognize the fallen love of the Deathlands as the magical illusion that it is. We see the goddess(es) performing the work of eternal yearning. We feel the higher love of the revelation that we are (always) already dead here, and we recognize the lament work of eternal yearning as Deathland purification for those of us who may ascend the *scala amoris*.

"I was distracted: madly did I kiss
The wooing arms which held me,
and did give
my eyes at once to death: but t'was to live,
To take in draughts of life
from the gold fount...

Our feet were soft in flowers."
~Keats "(The Vision of) Endymion," BK I (1817).

"then we emerged to see the stars again..."

I realize most people cling to the life of the body
and think of the life of the body as if it is something
to hold on to
as long as possible.
However, I have come to see it differently.
I now see embodiment as the physical dimension's inability
to, ultimately, contain us.
The journey of this body, as it dies,
is not our destruction. The journey of this body as it dies
is the spiritual experience of be-ing liberated...

Bibliography & Further Readings

Abraham, Lyndy. (2001). *A Dictionary of Alchemical Imagery*.
    Cambridge: Cambridge University Press.

Alderink, Larry J. (1981). *Creation and Salvation in Ancient Orphism*.
    Chico, CA: Scholars Press.

Allen, Michael J.B. (1984). *The Platonism of Marsilio Ficino: A Study
    of his Phaedrus Commentary, Its Sources and Genesis*.
    Berkeley, CA: University of California Press.

Ambelain, Robert. (1975). *Scala Philosophorum: Ou, la
    symbolique des outils dans l'art royal*. Paris: Éditions du
    Prisme.

Apuleius. (1995). *Cupid & Psyche*. E.J. Kenney (Ed. and
    Trans.). Cambridge, MA: Cambridge University Press.

Aristophanes. (1906). *The Birds of Aristophanes: Acted at
    Athens at the Great Dionysia B.C. 414*. B.B. Rogers (Trans.).
    London: George Bell & Sons.

_____. (2002). *Frogs. Assemblywomen. Wealth*. J.
    Henderson (Trans.). Cambridge, MA: Harvard University
    Press.

Aristotle. (1984). *On the Soul*. J.A Smith (Trans.). In J.
    Barnes (Ed.). *The Complete Works of Aristotle: The Revised
    Oxford Translation*. Vol. II. (pp. 641-692). Princeton, N.J.:
    Princeton University Press.

_____. (1924). *Metaphysics*. W.D Ross (Trans.). In J. Barnes (Ed.). *The Complete Works of Aristotle: The Revised Oxford Translation*. Vol. II. (pp. 1552-1728). Princeton, N.J.: Princeton University Press.

_____. (2009). *Nicomachean Ethics*. R. Crisp (Trans.). Cambridge: Cambridge University Press.

_____. (1950). *Physics*. W.D. Ross (Trans.). R. P. Hardie and R.K. Gaye (Rev.). In J. Barnes, (Ed.). *The Complete Works of Aristotle*. Vol. II. (pp. 315-446). New Jersey: Princeton University Press.

_____. (1995). *Poetics*. I. Bywater (Trans.). In J. Barnes (Ed.). *The Complete Works of Aristotle*. Vol. II. (pp. 2316-2340). New Jersey: Princeton University Press.

Ashmore, Elias. (1652/1967). *Theatricum chemicum Brittanicum*. London: Johnson Reprint Corporation.

Balz, Horst R., and Gerhard Schneider. (1990). *Exegetical Dictionary of the New Testament*. Grand Rapids, MI: Eerdmans.

Bardwick, J.M. (1971). *Psychology of Women*. New York: Harper & Row.

Bashō (2008). *Basho: The Complete Haiku*, J. Reichhold (Trans.). Tokyo: Kodansha International.

Baudrillard, Jean. (2008). *The Perfect Crime*. C. Turner (Trans.). London: Verso.

Bikerman, E. (1939). The Orphic Blessing. *Journal of the Warburg Institute* 2(4): 368-374.

Bibliography & Further Readings

Bilsker, Richard. (1997). Freud and Schopenhauer: Consciousness, the Unconsciousness, and the Drive Towards Death. *Idealistic Studies* 27: 79-90.

Blanchot, Maurice. (1981). *The Gaze of Orpheus*. L. Davis (Trans.). New York: Station Hill.

_____. (1988). *The Unavowable Community*. P. Joris (Trans.). New York: Station Hill.

Boethius. (1969). *The Consolation of Philosophy*. V.E. Watts (Trans.). London, Penguin Books.

Bostock, David. (2000). The Soul and Immortality in Plato's *Phaedo*. In G. Fine (Ed.) *Plato*. Oxford: Oxford University Press.

Bowman, Brady. (2012). Spinozist Pantheism and the Truth of "Sense Certainty": What the Eleusinian Mysteries Tell us about Hegel's Phenomenology. *Journal of History of Philosophy* 50(1): 85-110.

Brisson, Luc. (2008). How Philosophers Saved Myths: Allegorical Interpretation and Classical Mythology. C. Tihanyi (Trans.). Chicago, IL: University of Chicago Press.

Brody, B. (1970). Freud's case-load. *Psychotherapy: Theory, Research and Practice* 7: 8-12.

Browning, Robert. (1895). *The Complete Poetical Works of Browning*. Cambridge, MA: Houghton Mifflin Co.

Burkert, Walter. (1989). *Ancient Mystery Cults*. Cambridge, MA: Harvard University Press.

_____. (1962). *Orphism and Bacchic Mysteries: New Evidence and Old Problems of Interpretation*. Colloquy 28 of the Center for Hermeneutical Studies. W. Wilhelm Wuellner (Ed.). Berkeley, CA: Center for Hermeneutical Studies.

Cameron, A. (1938). *The Pythagorean Background of the Theory of Recollection*. Menasha, WI: George Banta.

Campbell, Joseph. (2008). *The Hero with a Thousand Faces*. Novato, CA: New World Library.

_____. (1979). *The Mysteries: Papers from the Eranos Yearbooks*. Cambridge, MA: Harvard University Press.

Cannon-Johnson, Patricia. (2010). The Neoplatonists and the Mystery Schools of the Mediterranean. In R. MacLeod (Ed.). *The Library of Alexandria: Centre of Learning in the Ancient World*. London: I.B. Tauris.

Cavalli, Thom F. (2010). *Embodying Osiris: The Secrets of Alchemical Transformation*. Wheaton, IL: Quest Books.

Cheak, Aaron. (2013). *Alchemical Traditions: From Antiquity to the Avant-Garde*. Melbourne, Australia: Numen Books.

Circlot, J.E. (1971). *A Dictionary of Symbols*. J. Sage (Trans.). London: Routledge.

Coleridge, Samuel Taylor. (2001). Dejection: An Ode. In J.C.C. Mays (Ed.). *The Collected Works of Samuel Taylor Coleridge*, Vol. XVI. (pp. 695-702). Princeton University Press.

Conrad, Peter. (2012). "Michael Haneke: There's no easy way to say this..." The Observer Nov. http://www.guardian.co.uk/film/2012/nov/04/michael-haneke-amour-director-interview.

Cornford, F.M. (1903). Plato and Orpheus. *The Classical Review* 17(9): 433-445.

Courdet, Allison. (1980). *Alchemy: The Philosopher's Stone.* Boulder, CO: Shambhala.

Dante, Alighieri. (1994). *The Inferno of Dante.* R. Pinsky (Trans.). New York: Farrar, Strauss & Giroux.

Deleuze, Gilles. (1994). *Difference & Repetition.* P. Patton (Trans.). New York: Columbia University.

_____. (1993). *The Fold: Leibniz and the Baroque.* T. Conley (Trans.). Minneapolis: University of Minnesota Press.

Derrida, Jacques. (1981). Plato's Pharmacy. In *Dissemination.* B. Johnson (Trans.). (pp. 61-172). London: The Athlone Press.

Detienne, Marcel. (1979). *Dionysos Slain.* M. Muellner and L. Muellner (Trans.). Baltimore, MD: The John Hopkins University Press.

Diamond, Stephen. (1996). *Anger, Madness, and the Daimonic.* New York, NY: SUNY Press.

Diehl, E. (1936). *Anthologia lyrica Graeca*, vol. I. Leipzig: Teubner.

Diogenes Laertius. (1925). *Lives of Eminent Philosophers*, vol. I. Cambridge, MA: Harvard University Press.

Edinger, Edward F. (1995a). *The Aion Lectures: Exploring the Self in C.G. Jung's* Aion. D.A. Wesley (Ed.). Toronto: Inner City Books.

_____. (1985). *Anatomy of the Psyche: Alchemical Symbolism in Psychotherapy*. LaSalle, IL: Open Court.

_____. (1995b). *The Mysterium Lectures: A Journey Through C.G. Jung's* Mysterium Coniunctionis. J.D. Blackmar (Ed.). Toronto: Inner City Books.

Edmonds, Radcliffe G. III. (2011).Who are you? A brief history of the scholarship. In R.G. Edmonds III (Ed.). *The 'Orphic' Gold Tablets and Greek Religion: Further along the Path*. (pp. 3-14). Cambridge: Cambridge University Press.

Eliot, T.S. (1944). *Four Quartets*. London: Faber and Faber.

_____. (2000). *The Waste Land*. M. Norton (Ed.). London: W.W. Norton & Co.

Entralgo, Lain. (1970). *The Therapy of the Word in Classical Antiquity*. New Haven, CT: Yale University Press.

Faraone, Christopher, A. (1999). *Ancient Greek Love Magic*. Cambridge, MA: Harvard University Press.

Ferrari, Giovanni R.F. (1987). *Listening to the Cicadas: A Study of Plato's Phaedrus*. Cambridge: Cambridge University Press.

Ficino, Marsilio. (1559). *Theologia Platonica de immortalitate animorum*. Paris: Apud Aegidium Gorbinum.

_____. (1981). *Marsilio Ficino and the Phaedran Charioteer*. M J.B. Allen (Trans. & Introduction). Berkeley, CA: University of California Press.

Fischer, Roland. (1971). A Cartography of the Ecstatic and Meditative States. *Science*, New Series, 174(4012): 897-904.

Foley, Helene P. (2013). *The Homeric "Hymn to Demeter"*. Princeton, NJ: Princeton University Press.

Franz, Marie-Louise von. (2015). *Alchemy: An Introduction to the Symbolism and the Psychology*. Toronto: Inner City Books.

_____. (1980). *Projection and Re-Collection in Jungian Psychology: Reflections of the Soul*. W.H. Kennedy (Trans.). London: Open Court.

_____. (1964). The Process of Individuation. In J. Freeman (Ed). *Man and His Symbols*. New York, NY: Dell Publishing.

_____. (1980). *The Psychological Meaning of Redemption Motifs in Fairytales*. Toronto: Inner City Books.

Girard, René. (1979). *Violence and the Sacred*. P. Gregory (Trans.). Baltimore, MD: The John Hopkins University Press.

Görner, Rüdiger. (2010). Rilke: A biographical exploration.
    In K. Leeder and R. Vilain (Eds.) *The Cambridge Companion
    to Rilke*. (pp. 9-26). Cambridge, Cambridge University
    Press.

Graf, Fritz. (1974). *Eleusis und Die Orphische Dichtung
    Athens in Vorhellenistischer Zeit*. Berlin: Walter de Gruyter.

Graf, Fritz., and Sarah Iles-Johnston. (2007). *Ritual Texts
    for the Afterlife: Orpheus and the Bacchic Gold Tablets*.
    London: Routledge.

Grass, William H. (1999). *Reading Rilke: Reflections on the
    Problems of Translation*. New York, NY: A.A. Knopf.

Grey, Alex. (1990). *Sacred Mirrors*. Rochester, VT: Inner Traditions.

Griswold, Charles L. (1986). *Self-Knowledge in Plato's*
    Phaedrus. New Have, CT: Yale University Press.

Guthrie, W.K.C. (1985). *The Greeks and their Gods*.
    Boston, MA: Beacon Press.

_____. (1979). *A History of Greek Philosophy, vol. II: The
    Presocratic Tradition from Parmenides to Democritus*.
    Cambridge: Cambridge University Press.

_____. (1993). *Orpheus and Greek Religion: A study of the
    Orphic Movement*. Princeton, NJ: Princeton University
    Press.

Hackforth, R. (1972). *Plato's Phaedrus*. Cambridge:
    Cambridge University Press.

Bibliography & Further Readings

Hadot, Pierre. (2002). *What is Ancient Philosophy?* M.
    Chase (Trans.). Cambridge, MA: Belknap Press.

Hansen, William. (2005). *Classical Mythology: A Guide to
    the Mythical World of the Greeks and Romans.* Oxford:
    Oxford University Press.

Harris, M.J. (1983). *Raised Immortal: Resurrection and
    Immortality in the New Testament.* London: Marshall.

Henderson, A. (1931). *The Wheel of Life: A Study of
    Palingenesis in Its Relation to Christian Truth.* London:
    Rider & Co.

Henderson, Joseph L., and Dyane N. Sherwood. (2003).
    Transformation of the Psyche: The Symbolic Alchemy of the
    Splendor Solis. New York: Routledge.

Henry, Elisabeth. (1992). *Orpheus with His Lute: Poetry
    and the Renewal of Life.* Carbondale, IL: Southern Illinois
    University Press.

Heraclitus. (1981). *The Art and Thought of Heraclitus: An
    Edition of the* Fragments *with Translation and
    Commentary.* C.H. Kahn (Trans.). New York: Cambridge
    University.

_____. (2003). *Fragments.* J. Hillman and B. Haxton
    (Trans.). New York: Penguin Books.

Hesiod. (2009). *Theogony and Works and Days.* M.L. West
    (Trans.). Oxford: Oxford University Press.

Hesse. Hermann. (1962). Dedication to Jung. H. Nagel
        (Trans.). *Spring*: 19.

Hillman, James. (1981). Alchemical Blue and the *Unio*
        Mentalis. *Sulfur* 1: 33-50.

_____. (2010). *Alchemical Psychology. Uniform Edition of*
        the Writings of James Hillman, vol. 5. Putnam, CT: Spring
        Publications.

_____. (2004). *Archetypal Psychology: A Brief Account.*
        Uniform Edition of the Writings of James Hillman, vol. 1.
        Putnam, CT: Spring Publications.

_____. (1989). *A Blue Fire*. New York: Harper and Row.

_____. (1992). *The Thought of the Heart and The Soul of the*
        World. Putnam, CT: Spring Publications.

_____. (1979). *The Dream and the Underworld*. New York,
        NY: Harper & Row.

_____. (1983). *Inter Views*. New York, NY: Harper & Row.

_____. (1996). *The Soul's Code: In Search of Character and*
        Calling. New York, NY: Random House.

Hirakawa, Akira. (1990). *A History of Indian Buddhism*.
        Delhi: Motilal Banarsidass.

Hoffman, Yoel. (Ed.). (1986). *Japanese Death Poems:*
        Written by Zen Monks and Haiku Poets on the Verge of
        Death. Boston: Charles E. Tuttle Publishing Co.

Hölderlin, Friedrich. (1980). *Poems & Fragments*. (Michael Hamburger, Trans.). Cambridge: Cambridge University Press.

Humphreys, Christmas. (Ed.). (1990). *The Wisdom of Buddhism*. London: Routledge.

Iamblichus. (1918). *Life of Pythagoras, Or Pythagoric Life: Accompanied by Fragments of the Ethical Writings of Certain Pythagoreans* and *A Collection of Pythagoric Sentences*. T. Taylor (Trans.). London: J.M. Watkins.

Irwin, L. (1991). The Orphic Mystery: Harmony and Mediation. In *Alexandria* (pp. 37-55). Grand Rapids, MI: Phanes Press.

Jacobi, Jolande. (1999). *Complex/Archetype/Symbol in the Psychology of C.G. Jung*. London: Routledge.

de Jáuregui, Miguel H., et al. (Eds.). (2011). *Tracing Orpheus*. Berlin: Walter de Gruyter.

Jung, C. G. (1968b). *Alchemical Studies*. R. F. C. Hull (Trans.). In H. Read et al. (Series Eds.), *The collected works of C.G. Jung*, Vol. 13. Princeton, NJ: Princeton University Press.

_____. (1969a). *Archetypes and the Collective Unconscious*. R. F. C. Hull (Trans.). In H. Read et al. (Series Eds.), *The collected works of C.G. Jung*, Vol. 9, Pt. 1. Princeton, NJ: Princeton University Press.

_____. (1969b). *Aion: Researches into the Phenomenology of the Self*. R. F. C. Hull (Trans.). In H. Read et al. (Series Eds.), *The collected works of C.G. Jung*, Vol. 9, Pt. 2. Princeton, NJ: Princeton University Press.

_____. (1977a). *C.G. Jung Speaking*. W. McGuire and R.F.C. Hull (Eds). Princeton, NJ: Princeton University Press.

_____. (1954). *Development of Personality*. R. F. C. Hull (Trans.). In H. Read et al. (Series Eds.), *The collected works of C.G. Jung*, Vol. 17. Princeton, NJ: Princeton University Press.

_____. (1961a). *Freud & Psychoanalysis*. R. F. C. Hull (Trans.). In H. Read et al. (Series Eds.), *The collected works of C.G. Jung*, Vol. 4. Princeton, NJ: Princeton University Press.

_____. (1977). Instinct and the Unconscious. *British Journal of Psychology* 10(1): 15-23.

_____. (1973). *C.G. Jung Letters*, vol. I: 1906-1950. R. F. C. Hull (Trans.). G. Adler and A Jaffé (Eds.). Princeton, NJ: Princeton University Press.

_____. (1976). *C.G. Jung Letters*, vol. II: 1951-1961. R. F. C. Hull (Trans.). G. Adler and A Jaffé (Eds.). Princeton, NJ: Princeton University Press.

_____. (1968c). *Man and his Symbols*. New York: Dell Publishing.

_____. (1961b). *Memories, Dreams, Reflections*. R. Winston and C. Winston (Trans.). New York, NY: Vintage Books.

_____. (1970). *Mysterium Coniunctionis.* R. F. C. Hull (Trans.). In H. Read et al. (Series Eds.), *The collected works of C.G. Jung,* Vol. 14. Princeton, NJ: Princeton University Press.

_____. (1988). *Nietzsche's Zarathustra: Notes of the Seminar Given in 193-1939,* vols. 1-2. J.L. Jarrett (Trans.). Princeton, NJ: Princeton University Press.

_____. (1985). *Practice of Psychotherapy.* R. F. C. Hull (Trans.). In H. Read et al. (Series Eds.), *The collected works of C.G. Jung,* Vol. 16. Princeton, NJ: Princeton University Press.

_____. (1968a). *Psychology and Alchemy.* R. F. C. Hull (Trans.). In H. Read et al. (Series Eds.), *The collected works of C.G. Jung,* Vol. 12. Princeton, NJ: Princeton University Press.

_____. (2014). *Psychology and Religion: West and East.* R. F. C. Hull (Trans.). In H. Read et al. (Series Eds.), *The collected works of C.G. Jung,* Vol. 11. Princeton, NJ: Princeton University Press.

_____. (1971). *Psychological Types.* R. F. C. Hull (Trans.). In H. Read et al. (Series Eds.), *The collected works of C.G. Jung,* Vol. 6. Princeton, NJ: Princeton University Press.

_____. (1970). *Structure & Dynamics of the Psyche.* R. F. C. Hull (Trans.). In H. Read et al. (Series Eds.), *The collected works of C.G. Jung,* Vol. 8. Princeton, NJ: Princeton University Press.

_____. (1956). *Symbols of Transformation*. R. F. C. Hull
        (Trans.). In H. Read et al. (Series Eds.), *The collected works
        of C.G. Jung*, Vol. 5. Princeton, NJ: Princeton University
        Press.

_____. (1977b).*The Symbolic Life: Miscellaneous Writings*.
        R. F. C. Hull (Trans.). In H. Read et al. (Series Eds.), *The
        collected works of C.G. Jung*, Vol. 18. Princeton, NJ:
        Princeton University Press.

_____. (1967). *Two Essays on Analytical Psychology*. R. F.
        C. Hull (Trans.). In H. Read et al. (Series Eds.), *The collected
        works of C.G. Jung*, Vol. 7. Princeton, NJ: Princeton
        University Press.

Jung, C. G., and Carl Kerényi. (1969). *Essays on a
        Science of Mythology: The Myth of the Divine Child and The
        Mysteries of Eleusis*. Princeton, NJ: Princeton University
        Press.

Jung, Emma. (1998). *Animus and Anima*. Putnam, CT:
        Spring Publications.

Kant, Immanuel. (2006). *Critique of the Power of
        Judgment*. P. Guyer and E. Matthews,
        (Trans.). Cambridge: Cambridge University Press.

_____. (2001). *Lectures on Metaphysics*. K. Ameriks and S.
        Naragon (Trans.). New York: Cambridge University Press.

_____. (1960). *Religion Within the Limits of Reason Alone*.
        T.M. Greene and H.H. Hudson. (Trans.). New York: Harper
        & Row.

Kennedy, Robert E. (1995). *Zen Spirit, Christian Spirit: The Place of Zen in Christian Life*. London: Bloomsbury.

Kenney, E.J. (1995). Introduction. In E.J. Kenney (Ed.). *Cupid & Psyche*. Cambridge, MA: Cambridge University Press.

Kerényi, Carl (1996). *Dionysos: Archetypal Image of Indestructible Life*. R. Manheim (Trans.) Princeton, NJ: Princeton University Press.

_____. (1967). *Eleusis: Archetypal Image of Mother and Daughter*. R. Manheim (Trans.). New York: Pantheon Books.

_____. (1974.). *The Gods of the Greeks*. London: Thames and Hudson.

_____. (1975). *Zeus and Hera: Archetypal image of father, husband, and wife*. Princeton, NJ: Princeton University Press.

Kierkegaard, Søren. (1983). *Fear & Trembling and Repetition*. H.V. Hong and E.H. Hong (Trans.). Princeton, NJ: Princeton University Press.

_____. (1980). *The Sickness Unto Death*. H.V. Hong and E.H. Hong (Trans.). Princeton, NJ: Princeton University Press.

Kingsley, Peter. (1995). *Ancient Philosophy, Mystery, and Magic: Empedocles and Pythagorean Tradition*. Oxford: Oxford University Press.

_____. (2004). *In the Dark Places of Wisdom*. Inverness,
    CA: The Golden Sufi Center.

Komar, Kathleen L. (2010). *The Duino Elegies*. In K.
    Leeder and R. Vilain (Eds.) *The Cambridge Companion to
    Rilke*. (pp. 80-94). Cambridge, Cambridge University Press.

Kugelmann, Robert. (1983). *The Windows of Soul*. J.
    Hillman (Series Eds.). *Studies in Jungian Thought*.
    Lewisburg, PA: Bucknell University Press.

Labouvi-Vief, Gisela. (1994). Psyche's Trials: The
    Transformation of Desire. In *Psyche & Eros*. (pp. 208-252).
    Cambridge: Cambridge University Press.

Lambspring, A. (1987). *The Book of Lambspring*.
    Somerset, UK: Llanerch Press.

Lampert, Laurence. (1995). *Nietzsche and Modern Times*.
    New Have, CT: Yale University Press.

Larson, Jennifer. (2001). *Greek Nymphs: Myth, Cult, Lore*.
    Oxford: Oxford University Press.

Leary, Timothy, Ralph Metzner, and Richard Alpert.
    (1990). *The Psychedelic Experience: A Manual Based on the
    Tibetan Book of the Dead*. New York: Citadel Press.

Linden, Stanton J. (2003). *The Alchemy Reader: From
    Hermes Trismegistus to Isaac Newton*. Cambridge
    University Press.

Linforth, Ivan M. (1973). *The Arts of Orpheus*. New York,
    NY: Arno Press.

Lobeck, Christian A. (1829). *Aglaophamus, sive de Theologiae Mysticae Graecorum Causis*. Königsberg: Regimonti Prussorum.

_____. (1827). *De Orphei Theogonia et Sermone Sacro*. Königsberg: Regimonti Prussorum.

Locke, Liz. (1997). Orpheus and Orphism: Cosmology and Sacrifice at the Boundary. *Folklore Forum* 28(2): 3-29.

Lowitz, Leza, Miyuki Aoyama, and Akemi Tomioka, (Eds. & Trans.). (2002). *A Long Rainy Season: Haiku & Tanka*. (*Contemporary Japanese Women's Poetry*, Vol. I). Berkeley, CA: Stone Bridge Press.

Lucas, D.W. (1977). *Aristotle: Poetics*. Oxford: Oxford University Press.

Macchioro, Vittorio D. (1930). *From Orpheus to Paul: A History of Orphism*. London: Henry Holt.

Manchester, Peter. (1986). The Religious Experience of Time and Eternity. In A.H. Armstrong (Ed.). *Classical Mediterranean Spirituality: Egyptian, Greek, Roman*. London: Routledge & Kegan Paul.

Martinec, Rüdiger. (2010). *The Sonnets to Orpheus*. In K. Leeder and R. Vilain (Eds.) *The Cambridge Companion to Rilke*. (pp. 95-112). Cambridge, Cambridge University Press.

McLean, Adam. (Ed.). (1980). *The Rosary of the Philosophers* (1550). Edinburgh: Magnum Opus Hermetic Sourceworks.

McGahey, Robert. (1994). *The Orphic Moment: Shaman to Poet-Thinker in Plato, Nietzsche, and Mallarmé*. New York, NY: SUNY Press.

Mead, G.R.S. (1896). *Orpheus*. London: Theosophical Publishing Society.

Mellers, Wilfrid. (1987). *The Masks of Orpheus: Seven Stages in the Story of European Music*. Manchester: Manchester University Press.

Miller, David L. (Ed.). (1995). *Jung and the Interpretation of the Bible*. New York, NY: Continuum.

_____. (1970) Orestes: Myth and Dream as Catharsis. In J. Campbell (Ed.) *Myths, Dreams, and Religion*. (pp. 26-47). New York: E.P. Dutton.

Mood, J.L. (1994). Introduction. (pp. 75-77). In *Rilke on Love and Other Difficulties: Translations and Considerations*. J.L. Mood (Trans.). New York, NY: W.W. Norton.

Morgan, Kathryn A. (2007). *Myth and Philosophy from the Presocratics to Plato*. Cambridge: Cambridge University Press.

Moriguchi, Yasuhiko. (1994). *The Song in the Dream of the Hermit: Selections from the Kanginshu*. Y. Moriguchi and D. Jenkins (Trans.). Seattle, WA: Broken Moon Press.

Mylonas, George E. (1974). *Eleusis and the Eleusinian Mysteries*. Princeton, NJ: Princeton Univ. Press.

Narby, Jeremy., and Francis Huxley, (Eds.). (2001). *Shamans Through Time: 500 Years on the Path to Knowledge*. New York: Putnam.

Nichols, Mary P. (2010). *Socrates on Friendship and Community: Reflections on Plato's* Symposium, Phaedrus, *and* Lysis. Cambridge: Cambridge University Press.

Nietzsche, Friedrich. (1989a). *Beyond Good & Evil: Prelude to a Philosophy of the Future*. W. Kaufmann (Trans.). New York: Vintage Books.

_____. (1967). *The Birth of Tragedy Out of the Spirit of Music*. W. Kaufmann (Trans.). New York: Vintage Books.

Novalis. (1997). *Philosophical Writings*. M.M. Stoljar (Trans.). Albany, NY: SUNY.

Orpheus. (1896). *The Mystical Hymns of Orpheus*. T. Taylor (Trans.). London: Bertram Dobell, Reeves and Turner.

Orr, Gregory. (2002). *Poetry as Survival*. Athens, GA: University of Georgia Press.

Ovid. (1986). *Metamorphoses*. A. D. Melville (Trans.). Oxford: Oxford University Press.

Pascal, Blaise. (1958). *Pensées*. W.F. Trotter (Trans.) New York: E.P. Dutton & Co., Inc.

Philalethes, Eirenaeus. (1678). *Ripley Reviv'd: or an Exposition upon Sir George Ripley's Hermetico-Poetical Works*. London: William Cooper.

Pieper, Josef. (1995). *Divine Madness: Plato's Case Against Secular Humanism*. L. Krauth (Trans.). San Francisco: Ignatius Press.

Plato. (1997a). *Apology*. G.M.A. Grube (Trans.). *Plato Complete Works*. John M. Cooper (Ed.). Indianapolis, IN: Hackett Publishing.

_____. (1997b). *Cratylus*. G.M.A. Grube (Trans.). *Plato Complete Works*. John M. Cooper (Ed.). Indianapolis, IN: Hackett Publishing.

_____. (1997c). *Gorgias*. G.M.A. Grube (Trans.). *Plato Complete Works*. John M. Cooper (Ed.). Indianapolis, IN: Hackett Publishing.

_____. (1997d). *Ion*. G.M.A. Grube (Trans.). *Plato Complete Works*. John M. Cooper (Ed.). Indianapolis, IN: Hackett Publishing.

_____. (1997e). *Laws*. G.M.A. Grube (Trans.). *Plato Complete Works*. John M. Cooper (Ed.). Indianapolis, IN: Hackett Publishing.

_____. (1997f). *Meno*. G.M.A. Grube (Trans.). *Plato Complete Works*. John M. Cooper (Ed.). Indianapolis, IN: Hackett Publishing.

_____. (1997g). *Phaedo*. G.M.A. Grube (Trans.). *Plato Complete Works*. John M. Cooper (Ed.). Indianapolis, IN: Hackett Publishing.

_____. (1997h). *Phaedrus*. A. Nehamas and P. Woodruff (Trans.). *Plato Complete Works*. John M. Cooper (Ed.). Indianapolis, IN: Hackett Publishing.

_____. (1997i). *Philebus*. A. Nehamas and P. Woodruff (Trans.). *Plato Complete Works*. John M. Cooper (Ed.). Indianapolis, IN: Hackett Publishing.

_____. (1997j). *Protagoras*. G.M.A. Grube (Trans.). *Plato Complete Works*. John M. Cooper (Ed.). Indianapolis, IN: Hackett Publishing.

_____. (1997k). *Republic*. G.M.A. Grube (Trans.). C.D.C. Reeve, (Rev.). *Plato Complete Works*. John M. Cooper (Ed.). Indianapolis, IN: Hackett Publishing.

_____. (1997l). *Sophist*. N.P. White (Trans). *Plato Complete Works*. John M. Cooper (Ed.). Cambridge: Hackett Publishing.

_____. (1997m). *Symposium*. A. Nehamas and P. Woodruff (Trans.). *Plato Complete Works*. John M. Cooper (Ed.). Indianapolis, IN: Hackett Publishing.

_____. (1997n). *Theaetetus*. M.J. Levett (Trans.). M. Burnyeat (Rev.). *Plato Complete Works*. John M. Cooper (Ed.). Indianapolis, IN: Hackett Publishing.

_____. (1997o). *Timaeus*. D.J. Zeyl (Trans). *Plato Complete Works*. John M. Cooper (Ed.). Indianapolis, IN: Hackett Publishing.

Plotinus. (1964). *The Essential Plotinus*. E.O'Brien (Trans.) Indianapolis, IN: Hackett Publishing.

Plutarch. (1914). *Lives, II: Themistocles*. B. Perrin (Trans.). Cambridge, MA: Harvard University Press.

Proclus. (1816). *Elements of Theology*. T. Taylor (Trans.). In *The Six Books of Proclus*. London: A.J. Valpy.

Prier, Raymond A. (1976). *Archaic Logic: Symbol and structure in Heraclitus, Parmenides, and Empedocles*. The Hague: Mouton Press.

Reinach, Salomon. (1909). *Orpheus: A general history of religions*. F. Simmonds (Trans.). London: William Heinemann.

Rilke, Rainer Maria. (2002). *The Book of Hours*. A.S. Kidder (Trans.). Evanston, IL: Northwestern University Press.

_____. (1991). *Briefe in zwei Bänden*. H. Nalewski (Ed.) Frankfurt am Main: Insel.

_____. (1942). *Duino Elegies*. J.B. Leishman & S. Spender (Trans.). New York: W.W. Norton.

_____. (1977). *Duino Elegies & The Sonnets to Orpheus*. A. Poulin, Jr. (Trans.). Boston: Houghton Mifflin Co.

_____. (1945). *Letters of Rainer Maria Rilke, vol. I (1892-1910)*. J.B. Greene and M.D.H. Norton. New York, NY: W.W. Norton.

_____. (1948). *Letters of Rainer Maria Rilke, vol. II (1910-1926)*. J.B. Greene and M.D.H. Norton. New York, NY: W.W. Norton.

_____. (2009). "Orpheus. Eurydice. Hermes," E. Snow
        (Trans.). *The Poetry of Rilke*. New York: North Point Press.

_____. (1989). "Orpheus. Eurydice. Hermes," S. Mitchell
        (Trans.). *The Selected Poetry of Rainer Maria Rilke*. New
        York: Vintage Press.

_____. (1989). *The Selected Poetry of Rainer Maria Rilke*. S.
        Mitchell (Ed. & Trans.). New York: Vintage Books.

Rouget, Gilbert. (1985). *Music and Trance: A Theory of the
        Relations between Music and Possession*. Chicago, IL:
        University of Chicago Press.

Ruck, Carl A. P. (1986). Mushrooms and Mysteries: On
        Aristophanes and the Necromancy of Socrates. *Helios* 8(2):
        1-28.

_____. (1981). Mushrooms and Philosophers. *Journal of
        Ethnopharmacology* 4(2): 179-205.

_____. (2006). *Sacred Mushrooms of the Goddess and the
        Secrets of Eleusis*. Berkeley, CA: Ronin Publishing.

Ruck, Carl A. P., and Danny Staples. (1994). *The World of
        Classical Myth: Gods and Goddesses, Heroines and Heroes*.
        Durham, NC: Carolina Academic Press.

Samuels, Andrew, Bani Shorter, and Fred Plaut. (1986). *A
        Critical Dictionary of Jungian Analysis*. London: Routledge
        & Kegan Paul.

Scalambrino, Frank. (2013). Filming the Impossible: Orpheus and
the Sense of Community in *Amour*. –Unpublished paper
presented at Film-Philosophy Conference: *Beyond Film*.
University of Amsterdam, The Netherlands.

_____. (2015). The Temporality of Damnation. (pp. 66-82). In R. Arp
and B.   McCraw, (Eds.). *The Concept of Hell*. New York:
Palgrave.

_____. (2016). *Meditations on Orpheus: Love, Death, and
Transformation*. Pittsburgh, PA: Black Water Phoenix Press.

_____. (2019). *Full Throttle Heart: The Rapture & Ecstasy of
Nietzsche's Dionysian Worldview*. Castalia, OH:
Magister Ludi Press.

_____. (2020). Being in the Continental Tradition:
Phenomenological Hermeneutics as Fundamental
Ontology. (pp. 39-82). In Li Vecchi, Scalambrino, and
Kovacs. *The Philosophy of Being in the Analytic,
Continental, and Thomistic Traditions: Divergence &
Dialogue*. London: Bloomsbury.

_____. (In Press, 2021). Rhythmic Chaos: The Time Sig-n-ature of
Ecstatic Spirit. (pp. TBD). In I. Joon and J. Weidenbaum,
(Eds.).   *The Mind in Nature: Extensions of Ecstatic
Naturalism*. Albany, NY: SUNY Press.

Scott, Charles E. (2001). *The Time of Memory*. Albany, NY: SUNY
Press.

Schelling, F.W.J. (2019) *On the Divinities of Samothrace*.
F. Scalambrino (Trans.). Castalia, OH: Magister Ludi Press.

Bibliography & Further Readings

Schwarz-Salant, Nathan. (1998). *The Mystery of Human Relationship*. London: Routledge.

Seznec, Jean. (1981). *The Survival of the Pagan Gods*. B.F. Sessions (Trans.). Princeton, N.J.: Princeton University.

Shelburne, Walter A. (1988). *Mythos and Logos in the Thought of Carl Jung: The Theory of the Collective Unconscious in Scientific Perspective*. Albany, NY: SUNY.

Small, Jocelyn Penny. (2001). *Wax Tablets of the Mind: Cognitive studies of memory and literacy in classical antiquity*. London: Routledge.

Steiner, Rudolf. (1910). *The Way of Initiation: Or, How to Attain Knowledge of Higher Worlds*. É. Schuré (Trans.). New York, NY: Macoy Publishing.

Sweeney, Leo. (1982). "Participation and the Structure of Being in Proclus' Elements of Theology. In R. Baine Harris (Ed.). *The Structure of Being: A Neoplatonic Approach*. (pp. 140-156). New York, NY: SUNY Press.

Taylor, Thomas. (1891). *The Eleusinian and Bacchic Mysteries*. New York, NY: J.W. Bouton.

_____. (1896). Introduction. (pp. vii-lv). In *The Mystical Hymns of Orpheus*. London: Bertram Dobell, Reeves and Turner.

Uždavinys, Algis. (2011). *Orpheus and the Roots of Platonism*. London: The Matheson Trust.

Vicari, Patricia. (1982). "Sparagmos: Orpheus among the Christians." (pp. 63-84). In J. Warden (Ed.). *Orpheus: The Metamorphoses of a Myth*. Toronto: University of Toronto Press.

Voss, Karen-Claire. (1990). The Hierosgamos Theme in the Images of the *Rosarium Philosophorum*. In Z.R.W.M. von Martels (Ed.). *Proceedings of the International Conference on the History of Alchemy at the University of Groningen*, April 17-19, 1989. Leiden: E.J. Brill.

Walker, D. P. (1958). *Spiritual and Demonic Magic: From Ficino to Campanella*. London: The Warburg Institute University of London.

Wasson, R. Gordon; Hofmann, Albert; Ruck, Carl A. P. (2008). *The Road to Eleusis: Unveiling the Secret of the Mysteries*. Berkeley, CA: North Atlantic Books.

Wedderburn, A.J.M. (1987). *Baptism and Resurrection: Studies in Pauline Theology against its Graeco-Roman Background*. Tübingen: Mohr.

Wind, Edgar. (1958). *Pagan Mysteries in the Renaissance*. New Haven, CT: Yale University Press.

Zuntz, Günther. (1971). *Persephone: Three Essays on Religion and Thought in Magna Graecia*. Oxford: Clarendon Press.

ABOUT THE TRANSLATOR

ꝏ   ☙

As of this publication, Frank Scalambrino has authored eight
books; additionally, he has produced one edited volume and one
anthology, authored over fifty professional peer-reviewed
publications, and taught over one hundred university-level courses,
including graduate-level courses in both
philosophy and psychology.

He is currently working as a Registered Psychotherapist
on the Adult Psychosis Unit at a psychiatric hospital
in Colorado Springs, Colorado.

His other translations include passages from the dialogues of Plato
and lectures, essays, letters, and poems by
Schelling, Schopenhauer, and Nietzsche.

He is the first person in the history of Western philosophy to
explicitly solve "the problem of 'non-being'"
as evidenced by his Doctoral Dissertation:
Non-Being & Memory: A Critique of Pure Difference.

Before age 27 he founded a Community Mental Health
Suicide Prevention Respite Unit and Clinical Intervention Center;
he subsequently received awards from multiple mental health
agencies across the local, county, and state levels of Ohio, and, in
the same year, was inducted into Chi Sigma Iota, the international
counseling honor society.

In determining his projects as an author, he believes:
"Empty is the word of that philosopher by whom no affliction of
men is cured. For as there is no benefit in medicine if it does not
treat the diseases of the body, so with philosophy, if it does not
drive out the affliction of the soul." ~Epicurus, "Fragment #54."

ꝏ   ☙